Praise for

Upside-Down Prayers for Parents

"Reading Lisa's book was a flashback to my own mothering years because my husband and I often carried similar petitions to our Father in heaven. We prayed our children would get caught in every lie every time. We asked God to allow them small fender-bender accidents as teens to temper their indestructible, immortal view of their lives. And when they experienced inevitable rejection, loneliness, and discouragement, we attempted to teach them that God wanted to use those hard experiences for their good. And they heard us speak these prayers, so when the answers came they knew Who was in control. *Upside-Down Prayers for Parents* will dispel the happily-ever-after deception that pervades our culture and will replace it with a solid bedrock view of God whose goal is our holiness, not our happiness—a foundational truth for everyday parenting. I plan to give Lisa's book to all my married children."

—BARBARA RAINEY, cofounder of FamilyLife Today and coauthor
of *Growing a Spiritually Strong Family*

"Lisa Bergren offers wise counsel, clear direction, and brilliant insights into how to pray in a way that shapes your child's character. Every mom needs this book! It will become a resource you will refer to often during your child's formative years and beyond."

—ROBIN JONES GUNN, author of the Christy Miller series
and *Praying for Your Future Husband*

"Lisa T. Bergren has crafted the perfect practical guide to enable parents to express the desires of their hearts, wrap them tightly in relevant Scripture, and send them soaring heavenward. The impact on their children—and quiet confidence they'll experience themselves—will reap sweet spiritual rewards for generations to come. If you've ever longed to trust God and entrust your kids to Him, this book is for you!"

—KAREN EHMAN, Proverbs 31 Ministries director of speakers
and author of six books, including *LET. IT. GO.: How to Stop
Running the Show and Start Walking in Faith*

"Lisa's upside-down prayers require a whole new level of faith and trust in Jesus. Reading this book and praying these prayers made me realize how tightly I was holding on to my children—and how much I needed to release them to God. These are exactly the prayers I've always wanted to pray for my children but could never find the words myself!"

—ERIN MOHRING, author of HomeWithTheBoys.net

"I love this book! These prayers confirm what I've learned in my twenty-three years as a mom: that sometimes it's the hard moments that bring about the heart-transformation in our kids. These are prayers to wrestle through—and find God in the midst of them. Highly recommended!"

—TRICIA GOYER, author of *Blue Like Play Dough: The Shape of Motherhood in the Grip of God*

"This is the perfect book for parents who want God's best for their children even when it's the difficult, more costly choice. Dive into this book and surrender your kids to Him. This book isn't a must *read;* it's a must *do*!"

—NICOLE O'DELL, author of the Hot Buttons series for parents

"Lisa T. Bergren describes this book as 'not a sweet and gentle devotional.' She's right. The prayers she asks us to offer on behalf of our kids are scary, raw, and honest. They demand our bravery. That's how I know they're good. And that's why I'll be praying these prayers along with her."

—MICHA BOYETT, author of Mama:Monk blog

"After reading these words and praying these prayers for thirty-one days, your heart can't help but be turned inside out. This book showed me the prayers I've always wanted to pray for my kids but just didn't know it. Health and favor merely scratch the surface of what I want for my kids; reliance on God, warrior faith, and deep assurance of God's love is what I really desire. Lisa T. Bergren leads us into examining our hearts so we can position our lives and prayers on the true blessing, redemption, power, and plans God has for our lives and the lives of our children."

—AMANDA WHITE, founder of ohAmanda.com and author of *Truth in the Tinsel: An Advent Experience for Little Hands*

Upside-Down
Prayers *for* Parents

31
Daring Devotions
for Entrusting
Your Child—*and*
Yourself—to God

Upside-Down
Prayers *for* Parents

Lisa T. Bergren

Best-Selling Author of *God Gave Us You*

WaterBrook
P R E S S

UPSIDE-DOWN PRAYERS FOR PARENTS
PUBLISHED BY WATERBROOK PRESS
12265 Oracle Boulevard, Suite 200
Colorado Springs, Colorado 80921

All Scripture quotations are taken from the Holy Bible, New International Version®,
NIV®. Copyright © 1973, 1978, 1984 by Biblica Inc.™ Used by permission of
Zondervan. All rights reserved worldwide. www.zondervan.com.

ISBN 978-0-307-95583-8
ISBN 978-0-307-95584-5 (electronic)

Copyright © 2013 by Lisa Tawn Bergren

Cover design by Mark D. Ford

Published in the United States by WaterBrook Multnomah, an imprint of the Crown
Publishing Group, a division of Random House Inc., New York.

WATERBROOK and its deer colophon are registered trademarks of Random House Inc.

Library of Congress Cataloging-in-Publication Data
Bergren, Lisa Tawn.
    Upside-down prayers for parents : 31 daring devotions for entrusting your
child—and yourself—to God / Lisa T. Bergren.—1st ed.
        p. cm.
    ISBN 978-0-307-95583-8—ISBN 978-0-307-95584-5 (electronic)
    1. Parents—Prayers and devotions. 2. Parent and child—Religious aspects—
Christianity. I. Title.
    BV4845.B47 2013
    242'.645—dc23

                                            2012034764

Printed in the United States of America
2013—First Edition

10 9 8 7 6 5 4 3 2 1

SPECIAL SALES
Most WaterBrook Multnomah books are available at special quantity discounts when
purchased in bulk by corporations, organizations, and special-interest groups. Custom
imprinting or excerpting can also be done to fit special needs. For information, please
e-mail SpecialMarkets@WaterBrookMultnomah.com or call 1-800-603-7051.

For Liv, Emma, and Jack—

May you know in your hearts
that the upside-down aspects of life
can always be made right-side-up
by the God who loves, loves, loves you,
through it all. Come what may.
—Mama

CONTENTS

Nurturing a Faith That Endures, Come What May

Here in southern Colorado, we recently witnessed the most devastating wildfire in state history. Hundreds of homes and thousands of acres burned. Smoke billowed up in an eerily colored, apocalyptic swirl, then descended over our city in a thick, brown haze that made your lungs hurt when you took a deep breath. Ash rained down, covering rooftops and yards—the sorrowful, wispy remains of *other* people's rooftops and yards. One elderly couple lost their lives. It was surreal, horrific to watch the flames march down the mountains like a dragon with a thousand tongues of fire, engulfing one house after another in fireballs. Over a thousand firefighters fought to keep it from taking other homes, yet it raced unabated across the forest floor, taking ridge after ridge.

In the aftermath, it broke our hearts to look upon the blackened remains of the once-verdant, beautifully green hills and valleys that border our town. But experts say that fire is actually *good* for the forest. (They'd prefer a manageable surface fire to a full-scale canopy fire like this one, but some-times the choice isn't theirs.) According to principles of forest management, what looks like devastation can actually be a gift, thinning out the dead material, opening up the tree can-opy, and enriching the soil with nutrients that aid new life.

Individuals who so tragically lost their entire neighbor-hood to the fire also sought the good that comes through loss. They sifted through the remains of their homes—a foot deep in ash—but they consistently mused about the gifts of life, of community, of people coming to their aid. It was heartwarm-ing to watch a spirit of unity unfold. Amid tragedy and crisis, people came together around a common focus: a desire to help others heal, survive, and rise again. And in our busy, separated, largely short-on-true-community lives, this was an-other gift we *all* counted among the ashes.

As Christians, we're called to take the lead when hard times hit. To stand and be counted among those who place their confidence in a God who is completely good, even when life feels bad. Yes, life is rough. At times, brutal. But it's also amazingly, achingly beautiful. Full of hope and potential and possibility. And if we want to raise children whose faith can thrive in difficult circumstances—children who live in a lov-ing, wholly trusting relationship with their God, who are able to see the beauty even in the midst of the fire and smoke, who remain alert for signs of hope amid the rubble—we have to model that kind of relationship with our God. *Come what may.*

As parents, we want to equip our children to be strong and courageous disciples. But we can only teach them what we already know for ourselves, right? So this devotional addresses both our personal relationship with God—to make sure we have his priorities clear in our heads and hearts—and our role as parents who seek to trust our loving God with our precious children, knowing he only seeks to be closer to them. *Come what may.*

We feel responsible to protect and shield our children from harm. So it seems odd to wish upon them anything but peace and prosperity. But if you're like me, the adults you admire—the people you'd like to befriend and emulate—are people who live life deeply, richly, and in a holy fashion, regardless of what life throws at 'em. They have the spiritual stamina to make it through the fires of difficulty and maintain a sense of optimism and hope. To press on through the darkness, which in turn somehow helps them better appreciate the light.

It's understandable and right to pray for our children's protection, health, and well-being. But too often, we slip into spiritual timidity. We like to stay in that safe zone—and we definitely prefer to see our children in that happy place, right? But if we wish to be warriors for Christ, resilient disciples of the Way, we're after more depth in discipleship, knowledge of the Holy, and a full-on trust of the One who loves our children best. And if we're to trust him with everything in us, we have to lay our lives—past, present, and future—in his hands. Perhaps most challenging, we have to lay our children's lives there as well.

This is not a sweet and gentle devotional. It wrestles with

thirty-one issues that will most likely drive us to our knees, praying ourselves or our children through them. But I believe God redeems the time, the effort, the pain, every time. And when you fully absorb these truths and make them a part of your prayer life, I believe you will see a harvest in your own life and in your children's. Because this is rich, dark, moist, fertile soil, post-fire stuff. *Growth* stuff. The kind of stuff that initially leaves you grasping for words and gasping for air. But after the smoke clears, when you can rise and take a deep, unencumbered breath, you will feel stronger for the experience, knowing that you've witnessed yet again the faithfulness of the One who loves you most.

The topics we'll be exploring touch on truths we want our children to learn sooner rather than later, truths that offer the security of knowing they will always be loved and will never be alone. And that, ultimately, is what all parents really want for their children, right? To that end, I've included little "discussion starters" at the end of each devotional, to aid you in sharing these perspective-shaping truths with your children.

I am praying for you this day, as you hold this devotional in your hands, that our Lord will hold you and your precious children in *his* hands. Peace upon you, sister and brother. May you be strong and courageous. May you make your God and your children proud by daring to know him better, each and every day, and by trusting him, regardless of what comes, so that your relationship with the Holy deepens, and your life grows richer in the process. Amen!

—LTB

I pray also that the eyes of your heart may be
enlightened in order that you may know the
hope to which he has called you, the riches of
his glorious inheritance in the saints, and his
incomparably great power for us who believe.

—Ephesians 1:18–19

Day **1**

I pray you'll get caught doing things wrong—and find the good and true path.

Show me your ways, O LORD,

teach me your paths;

guide me in your truth and teach me,

for you are God my Savior,

and my hope is in you all day long.

—Psalm 25:4–5

When kids are little, it's not such a big deal when they're caught doing wrong. The minor infractions of a preschooler—snitching a cookie without asking, shoving a friend, bending the truth, making a wall a massive art canvas—can even make parents roll their eyes (or laugh, behind closed bedroom doors, of course).

As children grow up, their "wrongs" have a bigger impact on them and those around them. The impulsive behaviors that were a little amusing in small children can become not-so-funny impulsive choices for teens. Things like shoplifting, physical fights, spreading false rumors, sleeping around, cheating.

And when they're adults? Left "uncaught," with no opportunity to learn the importance of self-discipline or experience the pain of consequences, wrong choices become a way of life. One detour after another can, over the years, lead to a seriously darker path. Often the choices gradually move from impulsive to premeditated.

I don't know about you, but I hate it when I have to face my children's sin. My hands are full just wrestling with my own. And when they get caught doing something wrong, I feel as if I have somehow fallen short, failed as a parent— failed them, society, and God. But the reality is that we are *all* sinful creatures. And brave, honest parents recognize this, even as they gaze upon their beautiful, gifted children—just as God looks at us. He sent his Son to save us all—every one of us.

We *all* struggle. For position. Authority. Love. Power.

Money. Security. We get ensnared by the world's definitions of happiness and success rather than submitting to becoming "schooled in the Lord's ways," which lead us—every time— to a far more satisfactory and meaningful life. Isn't it better that we get stopped short, *called out,* before we wander so deep into the forest of sin that we can't find our way out?

One at a time, choices shape and define our lives. Looking back over the years, I can pinpoint choices that could have gotten me fired from a job I loved, endangered a marriage I celebrate, cost a friendship, compromised my integrity, or even risked my life. I face such decisions every day, whether I recognize them or not. But God calls us to recognize them. And when I don't, I pray that he will stop me cold, shake me, smack me upside the head, and shout, "What do you think you're doing? Stop! Don't you see? Not this way. *That* way!"

Okay. I don't actually want him to be so rough. That's exactly my point. I want to hear and respond to his *whisper* rather than wait for him to start shouting. That way, I can leave the path that subtly slopes down toward darkness and get back on the path that leads to light.

We can choose to respond to correction before God shouts, just as our children can respond to our first warnings. You know how it goes: "Max honey, please stop doing that." "Max, please stop right now." "Max! Stop it! Go to your room!"

It takes a toll on us parents not only to catch our kids in their missteps but also to follow through with consequences and correction. Believe me, I know. It's hard work, this parenting gig. But for all of us, parents and kids alike, acknowledging the fact we've been on the wrong path—and seeking God's redirection—is the first step toward the path of peace and wholeness. So let's pray that we *all* may be caught, and *early,* when we set out on the wrong paths. And have the courage to quickly change direction.

> *Father God, I want to follow you so closely that I cannot choose anything but what you want for me, yet I often get off track. And I'm supposed to be the role model for my child! Help me to pay better attention to you and notice you "catching me" as soon as I step on the wrong path. And please give me the courage and insight both to help catch my child and to guide him in the way you want us all to live. Redirect us, Lord. Amen.*

MAKING IT PERSONAL

Have you recently made a bad choice, one that's taken you down a path you know is wrong? Have you hurt somebody, perhaps even yourself? Let's get after it—by going to the Savior who sees, and forgives, all. Pray for his direction and write below what you think he's telling you to do to get back on track.

_____

_____

_____

_____

_____

_____

_____

_____

_____

MAKING IT RELEVANT

For younger children: Do you ever notice people around you making wrong choices? What's an example? What do you think God thinks about that?

For older children: I'm trying to be a better listener when God speaks. He often prompts me to pause before a big decision, before it's too late—when I can make the best one. Have you ever felt him caution or encourage you, deep inside? What did that sound like or feel like?

Day 2

I pray you'll fail in things that don't matter—and learn to seek what matters to God.

If the LORD delights in a man's way,
    he makes his steps firm;
though he stumble, he will not fall,
    for the LORD upholds him with his
        hand....
Turn from evil and do good;
    then you will dwell in the land forever.

—Psalm 37:23–24, 27

As parents, we don't like to see our kids fail—even if failure might provide just the reality check they need. I'm no scientist, but I think we're biologically programmed to try to protect our children from the hurt and pain that failure brings, even if it means pushing them to persevere in something that lies outside their strengths and long-term interests. We make the tone-deaf kid practice piano. We book time at the batting cages for a child who's better suited to the library than the ball field. We insist on the advanced-placement class, thinking it will aid on college applications, even though the pressure makes the child (and therefore the whole family) miserable all year.

Factor in the reality that we somehow think a child's failure is a reflection on us—*What will people think of me if my child fails?*—and we actually exacerbate the problem. We pressure our children to achieve success at all costs, sometimes to the detriment of something more valuable. That isn't to say we shouldn't encourage our kids to do their best and to follow through on their commitments. I'm not advocating dropouts. I'm advocating dropping things that don't matter and really winnowing down to the things that move God, the things that should move us too. I'm challenging us to weather the What Will They Think of Me storm in favor of trusting—truly trusting—the Father with our kids.

God revels in the beautiful song, a sweet home run on a summer's day, excellence in academics. I'm certain of it. But not everyone is a gifted pianist, an all-star ballplayer, or the genius in the class. The Father loves it when our gifting shines.

But too often, we ignore *his* gifting—something promised to us all because our character is what matters most to him. How we use his gifts to show his love and glorify him is far more important than what we accomplish. But how often do we let that truth direct where we invest our time and energy?

Even as adults, in the jungles of our lives, we catch sight of one exotic, rare bird after another and think, "If I can catch it, it will bring me joy [or fame, money, satisfaction]." We then bushwhack off into the green, swinging a machete to blaze our way through, only to find we've ended at the edge of a fearsome canyon, the bird hopelessly out of reach. We've chased after the world's definition of success and fulfillment rather than the things that matter to the Father.

The things that matter to God often take the shape of service, support, empathy, mercy, grace, and love rather than medals, trophies, and report cards. And you know what? We people of the Way are all gifted in those things. Every one of us. If we exercise those gifts, in his name, *there is no way we can fail.*

So why do we press or even enable our kids to continue on paths that ultimately won't matter? If they invest time and energy on those things, they're inevitably missing something else. Possibly something greater. Let's not be parents who encourage our children to grasp at shiny trinkets that reflect a bit of the light rather than reaching for the Light itself. Such things only distract them, temporarily mesmerize them, and keep them from noticing when God beckons.

That doesn't mean that they won't elect to grab hold of

that shiny trinket anyway. Sometimes we have to finish chasing the temptations, grasping at the illusions, before we can see the truth. To fail—to get to the end of *ourselves*—before we finally look to him and ask him what's important to him and how we might serve. When that happens, we quit fighting our way through the jungle, exhausting ourselves and ultimately making little progress of note. And we find we are already right where God wants us—ready to serve him.

> *Lord, forgive me for interfering with my kids. For pushing my values on them rather than encouraging them to understand yours. For taking on their failures as a reflection of my inadequacy. Help me to recognize them as your children first and treat them as such, trusting them to your hands and encouraging them to seek you out, whether they're enjoying triumph or stinging from failure. When my children are chasing success down paths that lead away from you, I trust you enough to let them fail and lead them toward a more fulfilling life. We need you, Lord. Keep our eyes on you and our ears tuned to hear your call. Help us stay focused on you, and not on all the ways our world distracts us from following your will. Amen.*

MAKING IT PERSONAL

Are you struggling with a failure, past or present? Are you failing because you're chasing something God doesn't support? Or are you failing at something God wants because something else is robbing you of the time and energy you need to make this a priority? Write your thoughts here:

_____

_____

_____

_____

_____

_____

_____

MAKING IT RELEVANT

For younger children: What do you think God has made you good at doing? You know what's even more important to him? Who you are. I see that you're good at _____.
[Loving, serving, caring, listening, following through—you fill in the blank.]

For older children: What's the worst "Fail" you've seen or experienced lately? Why do you think God sometimes lets us fail? What do you think is more important to him than what we do?

Day **3**

I pray you'll have to forgive someone who doesn't deserve it—and find the peace that forgiveness brings.

Then Peter came to Jesus and asked, "Lord, how many times shall I forgive my brother when he sins against me? Up to seven times?"

Jesus answered, "I tell you, not seven times, but seventy-seven times."

—Matthew 18:21–22

We have inborn fair-o-meters, don't we? An innate sense of justice that makes us want everyone to be governed by the same rules. Even my teens cry, "That's not fair!" when something seems off to them, whether it be that their sibling got an extra scoop of ice cream or their best friend gets to do something that we can't swing financially.

And when someone tramples upon our hearts, our rights, our property, or our loved ones—and then doesn't even have the decency to feel bad about it...*humph!* We seriously struggle with get-even thoughts. (I've certainly had *you'll-have-to-crawl-on-your-knees-before-I-forgive-you* thoughts.) Deeper hurts bring even deeper reactions—rage, gaping emotional wounds, bitterness.

As parents, we often get even *more* offended and indignant when others hurt our children. We want things made right—immediately! We want an apology! We long for the wrongdoer to be brought low and our child to be returned to...*Oh. Yeah.* To a pedestal?

At some point, we have to recognize that we all disappoint others, betray others, hurt others—whether or not we realize it. Ephesians 4:32 tells us that we've all been forgiven by God for Christ's sake. Jesus's sacrifice for us is Grace, personified. And when we extend grace to others—the same grace we've been given—*and teach our children to do the same,* we begin to understand a whole other layer of our Savior's love. That realization frees us to embrace more peace and freedom in our lives, rather than cling to anger and bitterness.

We are to be like Jesus in every way possible, to emulate him. Think about it. Did he ever hold back? Even on the cross, he granted absolution, clearing the way for the criminal at his side to enter paradise, a forgiven man (Luke 23:42–43). If we trust him to see justice done, in his time, in his way, then why are we trying to usurp his place? Only he has ultimate authority in such matters. And in that powerful example, he didn't wait for the criminal to wallow in his guilt, to demonstrate worthiness, to prove himself. *All that guy had to do was express his belief in the King's authority and power.*

So who are we to require groveling before we offer grace?

To withhold forgiveness is to take on a role that belongs only to our Savior, to try and wrestle his crown away from him and put it on our own heads. By contrast, offering forgiveness acknowledges two important and universal realities: First, we're constantly in need of forgiveness ourselves—no less than anyone who has sinned against us. And second, forgiveness benefits those who freely grant it, even if the perpetrator doesn't confess.

These are hard truths for us to accept and even harder for our children to comprehend. We frequently ask them to apologize when they do wrong, and so understandably, they want to hear Ronnie Wrongdoer say he's sorry. *It's only fair.*

All too easily we get caught up in the injustice, the pain, the frustration rather than relinquishing it to the ultimate Judge of sinners, the Healer who stands ready to administer balm to our wounds and wrap us in peace. But the wise know that refusing to forgive Ronnie Wrongdoer hurts no one more than us. That time spent lost in the swirl of resentment is time we've missed living in peace and joy. If we can teach our kids to move beyond the hurt, trusting God to see justice served rather than demanding things be "made right, right now," they will learn to live not in turmoil, agitation, and bitterness, but in peace and joy. The forgiven and forgiving life we're meant to live. A life focused not on the wrongs of others but on the wonder of grace.

Savior, I've put myself in your place, over and over again. I want to be the Enforcer of Justice, when, at root, I am weak, fallible, a sinner myself. Somehow, use me to model forgiveness for my children, so that they never grow roots of bitterness. Help my children to recognize their own need for forgiveness and to demonstrate compassion and mercy to those who seem most undeserving. I submit my children to your care, along with the hurtful situations and hurtful people they will encounter. I lay them at your feet, trusting that you will see all injustice resolved, in your time. All I am to do is forgive, as you forgive us. And I do so now... Amen.

MAKING IT PERSONAL

Do you believe Jesus died on the cross for all? For *all*? Do you
believe he forgives us all and is the ultimate Judge? And yet,
are you holding on to the wrong someone else has done you?
If so, write out your prayer of confession here:

_____

_____

_____

_____

_____

_____

_____

_____

_____

_____

MAKING IT RELEVANT

For younger children: When did you recently have to forgive a
friend? Was it hard?

For older children: What's the hardest thing you've ever had to
forgive? How does holding back forgiveness keep us in our
own kind of prison?

Day 4

I pray you'll weep—and feel
free to express both tears of
anguish and tears of joy.

Those who sow in tears
    will reap with songs of joy.
He who goes out weeping,
    carrying seed to sow,
will return with songs of joy,
    carrying sheaves with him.

—Psalm 126:5–6

For most of two decades, the only times I saw my husband cry was when I walked down the aisle in a wedding gown, when I birthed him a baby, and when a baseball icon retired. While Tim and I were raised by loving parents, I think our generation—especially the boys—absorbed the message that we should "buck up" and "never let 'em see you cry." But in the last couple of years, Tim's been giving in to the tears, crying with me during poignant stories on the news or even—wait for it—during Hallmark commercials.

Now me, I've always been a feeler. But the older I get, the more of a blubbering mess I become. These days I'm pretty much A Mess, as my southern sister says. Seriously. I have to carry tissues 24/7 and have them in every room of my house, and it isn't due to allergies. It's because more and more, I'm given to tears.

It's not that I'm often sad—only a few of the tears I've cried in the last year were due to disappointment or sorrow. It's that I'm often *moved*…by something important, by someone else's triumphant story, by joy. And I welcome the tears, because feeling *moved* means I'm feeling *life*. Not operating on autopilot but truly feeling the moments that matter.

For the most part, my kids giggle and roll their eyes when they see me crying over the heartwarming news story or the poignant scene in a movie. But I've noticed that in being free with my tears, I've given my kids permission to be free with theirs too. Even my little second grader is given to happy tears on occasion, which makes me all the happier; to share such deep emotion for a moment draws us closer together. And I believe the ability to give expression to their feelings will serve them well in the future.

Our impulse is to stop our kids from crying, right? Depending on the circumstances, we immediately try to make it all better or we urge them to "suck it up" and quit crying. Tears generally make us uncomfortable, and we want to move our children quickly past their emotional outbursts.

But tears are the signs of an open heart. We see weeping and wailing throughout Scripture. And I love the story of Joseph's reunion with his brothers, after years of trial and pain in a land far from home. We would understand if his heart was hardened, if he refused to cry and just sought to repay the heartache they'd inflicted on him. (Okay, so he gives them a *little* grief.) But in the end, he opens both his arms and his heart, and the result is weeping—in front of his brothers, as well in the privacy of his room (Genesis 45:1–2, 14–15). It's as if a pressure-capped pool of both joy and sorrow is tapped, and the two emotions seep to the surface.

A few weeks ago, I was in my teen's room, praying for her because she was feeling far from God. As I did so, I felt the rush of the Holy Spirit in the room. The tears flowed, which totally freaked her out, of course. She thought I was hurt or "super sad." But it was more that I felt *her* hurt, her ache, her emptiness—bore the weight of her burdens, in the moment. And what is more, I felt the Father's desire to heal, ease, and fill her heart.

This has become the norm when I'm in intense prayer, intense communion with the Spirit. The rush of him, the knowledge of his presence. Tears are just one way I relinquish my pride and set aside myself, giving free rein to the God of all emotion. If I am his temple, who am I to cordon off a section?

He created in us the capacity to feel the dark chasm of despair, the penetrating light of hope, the breath-stealing wrench of loss, the heart-soaring moments of joy. To not allow ourselves to feel it all—good and bad—is to miss the breadth of life he offers us. And if we want our children to be free with their emotions, we must first show them how.

Creator, I like to look good. I confess I don't like it when others look down at me for being weak or overly emotional—even if it's my own children. But I know that in setting aside my pride, I allow more of you to fill me. And I want you to use me, Father, to reach my children for you with the message that you planted our emotions in us for your good purposes. Help them to see that you are fully trustworthy, whether they're feeling anguish or joy. Soften our hearts. Make us unafraid to show the world that you are the Ruler of everything in our lives, from the inside out. Amen.

MAKING IT PERSONAL

Is there a wall inside you that makes you hesitate to cry in front of others, whether for joy or sadness? Can you define what it is, or why it might be there?

_____

_____

_____

_____

_____

_____

_____

_____

_____

MAKING IT RELEVANT

For younger children: What makes you cry? Do you know that it's okay to cry?

For older children: When was the last time you cried? Do you think of crying as weakness? Why do you think that is?

Day 5

I pray you'll get lost—and
discover you have the
Compass within to help
you find your way.

Send forth your light and your truth,
  let them guide me;
let them bring me to your holy mountain,
  to the place where you dwell.

—Psalm 43:3

Olivia, our eldest, has lived in the same town for most of her life, but she doesn't know where anything is. This became clear when she began driver's training, and we had to talk her through every turn. I was the same way at her age. Until I was the responsible one behind the wheel, I never really paid attention to street names or how to get from point A to point B.

Not that I have the best sense of direction even now. All my life, I've lived next to location-orienting mountains and wondered how people in the desert or plains figure out which way is which. (Clearly, plains people have gifting I do not.)

Recently, I took my daughter Emma to Rome, and our directional confusion became a standing joke: "Oh, look! There's the Pantheon!" No matter where we were going, we seemed to circle back to that landmark. It happened twelve times in ten days. I'm serious. Quit laughing.

I found myself wishing we'd brought a compass along— it would've helped us so much. Or that we had a smart phone with a GPS. But without such gadgets on hand, we started to pay attention to the direction of the sun. Which side of the buildings we wanted it on when we were heading north or south, east or west. And gradually, we took fewer detours, logged fewer miles. Because we weren't relying on our own fallible instinct but on clues to the Creator's direction.

Our culture applauds people Who Know Where They're Going. Goal-oriented kids get bright, shiny stars. Children with a good sense of external "direction" and a list of accomplishments are admired. And we pat ourselves on the back when those kids are our own. Because, after all, we're the ones who taught them to navigate efficiently. To figure out where they want to go in life and how to get there.

But have we taught them to plot a course for success by relying on themselves—what *they* know and can do—rather than on what the Spirit knows and shows them to do?

The most "lost" I ever felt in my life was in the year after college. As a bartending ski bum, I gradually understood that I was in deep depression, having slipped my Christian moorings and set sail on a worldly sea. The weekend that followed that realization was filled with tears and a trembling awareness that I was alone, utterly lost in the darkness.

But I wasn't alone. Not really. As my pastor says, when we become believers, it's like we're on one end of a very long bungee cord and Jesus is on the other. We might wander far and wide, but never farther or wider than he can reach. Not when he abides within us.

Acknowledging my willful wandering, confessing my sin, crying out to my Deliverer brought me back on track as surely as Liv finding the right street to get her home or us finding the right route in Rome. He is our internal Compass, the sun on our shoulder, pointing, again and again, to True North. All we have to do is pay attention to his direction.

So we're endeavoring to teach our children this skill while they're still relatively safe at home, rather than out in the wide world. We allow them to make choices, and then, when it's clear they've gotten just a bit lost, we review, helping them trace their route back, like a disoriented driver, to where they made the first wrong turn. Often that leads them to a "think vs. know" point—"I *thought* I knew the way..." Which inevitably allows us to encourage them back to the way we all *know* is right, the way made clear by that internal Compass.

> *Lord, you know I like to feel as if I know exactly where I am and where I'm going at all times. Please help me relinquish that need for an illusion of control. Help me to teach my children to hear your voice and sense your direction. Let them experience the confusion of getting just lost enough that they'll stop trusting their own instincts and instead seek your guidance. Help them to recognize when they're on a road that isn't one you want them on. Hold our hands, Lord. Don't let go! Lead us in, lead us out, lead us away, lead us forward. Guide us, always. Amen.*

MAKING IT PERSONAL

Are you in the place God wants you right now—physically, mentally, emotionally, spiritually, relationally? If not, where do you think he is leading you?

_____

_____

_____

_____

_____

_____

_____

_____

MAKING IT RELEVANT

For younger children: Why do you think I like you to hold my hand when we're in a crowded place?

For older children: Do you remember how it felt, when you were little, to hold my hand through a crowded place? Do you know that God holds our hands like that, even now? How do you think we can figure out which way he wants us to go?

Day **6**

I pray you'll sweat—and learn what it means to work hard for what's worthwhile.

The one who sows to please his sinful nature, from that nature will reap destruction; the one who sows to please the Spirit, from the Spirit will reap eternal life. Let us not become weary in doing good, for at the proper time we will reap a harvest if we do not give up.

—Galatians 6:8–9

I'm rather un-fond of sweating. In the summer I walk as early in the morning as I can so I don't perspire as much. It doesn't help that, with even a little exertion, my face gets beet red and people worry that I'm having a heart attack.

By contrast, my friend is into hot yoga—which to me sounds like it belongs on the devil's menu list for his own private spa, right along with the sweltering sauna and the hot, burning stones pre-massage. (I know, I know—those are probably your favorite ways to relax!). But my Hot Yoga Friend swears that when she's done, she feels "more flexible, lighter, focused, and relaxed."

Despite her cheering and chiding, I'm not yet ready to don my own sweatband and yoga pants to Bring On the Sweat in a room where the thermostat is set at 102 degrees. I'd probably sweat enough just doing regular yoga. But I think I understand what she's describing.

Over time, the things that have grown me, stretched me—the things that, in retrospect, have shaped me more fully into who I was created to be—have been those who hurt a little (or a lot) to obtain. Meaningful relationships. Strides in my faith life. Professional accomplishments. I'm guessing you would say the same.

But as parents we still tend to point our kids toward the easiest way, don't we? We often advocate taking the path of least resistance. It's one thing to work superhard ourselves, but we squirm when we watch our children struggle, especially when it costs them something to work toward a goal. We cringe when they strain under the effort—emotionally, mentally, physically, spiritually. We can tolerate that struggle for a bit. But if we sense it's become too much of a burden, our inclination is to run and rescue. We swoop in to lift their load.

Certainly, at times it's appropriate to step in. But too often we react impulsively rather than prayerfully considering what growth God might have intended for our children in the process. Is it his goal to grow their emotional, mental, physical, or spiritual muscles? Might a little sweat, struggle—even pain—better accomplish his objectives for maturing our children or developing particular strengths for what lies ahead in their lives?

The things in life that come easily are rarely the things that bring us fulfillment and joy. Superficial relationships. Stuff that money can buy. Activities that fill our days but don't make life fulfilling. These aren't the things that we'll value over time or remember as turning points, defining events that shaped our lives.

As children of the King, we are not meant to float with the current of this world or to follow the broad and gentle path of ease. We are called to strive toward excellence in all that we are and do. We accomplish this not through our own strength but by delving deep into his. Only as we—and our children—attempt the hard things he's led us to attempt, do we discover how he's gifted us to serve him. And then we're inspired to put forth even more sweat-producing efforts to see those goals through to completion. Persevering through the struggle, we feel the satisfaction of accomplishing something that matters.

Lord of All, you know I'm inherently lazy. I prefer to take the shortest, easiest course rather than hiking the road you lay before me. And you know that sometimes, in my attempt to help my children, I minimize what you seek to do in their lives. Help me to trust you and seek your guidance before I move in to help. Let my children experience the exhilaration of pressing on to serve you when the task seems too hard. Give them the strength to endure through the sweat-drenching deserts, over the sweat-inducing climbs, as well as through the sweat-drying downhill stretches. Give all of us your vision and heart, and let us not waver. Amen.

MAKING IT PERSONAL

Is God asking you to do something that you fear will be too hard? Are you worried about what it will demand of you mentally, emotionally, spiritually, physically? What is he telling you now about that?

_____

_____

_____

_____

MAKING IT RELEVANT

For younger children: What is something you had to work hard to get? Was it worth it? Why or why not?

For older children: What's a goal you have right now? What will it take to reach it? Do you think God supports that goal? Why or why not?

Day **7**

I pray you'll get so weary you give up—and learn that with submission comes strength.

Do you not know?
Have you not heard?
The LORD is the everlasting God,
the Creator of the ends of the earth.
He will not grow tired or weary,
and his understanding no one can
fathom.
He gives strength to the weary
and increases the power of the weak.

—Isaiah 40:28–29

Despite my aversion to sweat, I think of myself as pretty strong. I come from sturdy stock: Swiss-German on one side, Norwegian and Scottish on the other. I identify with my ambitious, tenacious ancestors, who set sail for America, staked homesteads, plowed fields, bred horses, and led everything from Sunday schools to hospital wards and Grange halls. They raised children and held marriages together while surviving financial devastation, death, drug addictions, and detours. My ancestors found their place in this world and, gradually, peace and prosperity, even when facing significant challenges.

I sit up straighter as I write those words. I'm fiercely proud of My People. Proud to carry their blood in my veins. Proud to be a birth-certified Thompson-Leitch-Johnson-Grosswiler-Bergren. Can you just see me, waving my combined family herald, declaring my mutt-dom with glorious, sweeping moves on the horizon as the sun sets behind me? Now add to that heritage the fact that my parents raised an optimist. And between the powerful blood I carry and the powerful belief that I can do all, I've accomplished a lot.

I'm cringing as I write *those* words. It pains me to admit it, but even in my middle age, well along this road of discipleship, so much of how I approach life is still *all about me*. Far too often I'm consumed with thoughts about the power of me. What I have done. What I can do. I still find myself believing that if I can just pick myself up one more time, stretch a bit farther, put in a little more effort, invest more, I can make whatever I want happen.

Part of it is the American Dream. Part of it is a lie I've willingly swallowed. My People weren't the submissive sort. And neither am I. My take-charge attitude has at times undermined my ability to live by faith, prompting me to view God's way as a fallback plan, rather than plan A.

I've passed on to my children that spirit of tenacity. I've affirmed the mantra of *The Little Engine That Could* ten times more often than I've taught them to seek out God's wisdom and rely on his strength. I've taught them to push through, to go after what they want. And then I get irritated when they press for their own way rather than submitting to my parental wisdom. My youngest begs for a new action figure when I know that he has twenty like it at home. My eldest presses me to spend her savings on a day at the amusement park when I know she needs to save for a mission trip. My middlest insists she can handle a sleepover for the third night in a row, when I know it'll inevitably leave her exhausted and probably sick.

In submitting—once I've finally worn down their arguments—my eldest discovers she's closer to her savings goal; my middlest falls asleep early and finds she feels great the next morning; my youngest remembers a favorite action figure he hasn't played with for a long time and digs through his toy chest to find it. What I hope they're discovering in those everyday occurrences is a bit of the greater spiritual lesson—that we're to be tenacious about following God's lead rather than our own agenda. That we actually *gain* by "giving up" and "giving in" to God's greater plan.

We Christians love Philippians 3:14 and the idea of

pressing on toward the goal. But too often it's not God's goal we're pursuing but our own. If we back up a few lines for the full context, we discover that the goal Paul spoke of was "to know Christ and the power of his resurrection and the fellowship of sharing in his sufferings" (verse 10).

Yeah. We don't like to quote that part of the passage very often. And yet, what greater goal can we have than to know Christ so intimately that we're willing to suffer for him? To fully embrace the power of his resurrection is to be so deeply aware of his sacrifice that our egos are consumed by it, our souls infused with it, and our hearts are both broken and empowered by it. But to live in such a way, we must acknowledge that our lives are not our own, but his, to rule. If we wish to truly be strong, we begin pursuing his goals, in submission, on our knees. Lifting our hands, opening our hearts, saying, "I am yours, Father. Use me as you choose."

In doing so, we discover that submission leads to a limitless, God-fueled life, one that carries us to places we could never go on our own meager, limited reserves.

God of Strength, you are mighty. Forgive me for relying on my own strength, for looking to you last, out of desperation, rather than first. Help me get this straight in my head and model for my children what it means to live a fully submitted life. Help them to recognize it early—what it means to be yours, wholly.

> *I submit, Lord. I release control. I wait on you to lead me, in all things and in all places and with all people. And I ask you to help me return to those promises every time I grow weary because I've been pursuing my own passions. Amen.*

MAKING IT PERSONAL

In what part of your life do you struggle with submitting to God's strength rather than relying on your own?

_____

_____

_____

_____

_____

MAKING IT RELEVANT

For younger children: Why do you think we like to be in charge or be the leader?

For older children: Do you think God wants us to rely on him, or does he want us to be self-reliant? What does it mean when Paul says, "For when I am weak, then I am strong" (2 Corinthians 12:10)?

Day **8**

I pray you'll encounter battles—and find God is your greatest ally.

Therefore put on the full armor of God, so that when the day of evil comes, you may be able to stand your ground, and after you have done everything, to stand.

—Ephesians 6:13

T he battles are all around us. Temptation. Disease. Discouragement.

Day in and day out, we keep our heads down, hoping we can evade the struggle. Escape it. But sometimes the battle comes to our door or sneaks into the house before we even realize the enemy has set his sights on us. And in facing the battle, we quickly grow desperate, as if we've been stripped and beaten. By day we fight panic and by night we fight sleeplessness.

Battle-times are painful times. But they also are defining moments, providing opportunities to identify more clearly what we stand for…and what we do not. When we're challenged, truly challenged, to fight for the things we deem most important—faith, family, friendship, life itself—we recognize that everything else is transitory, temporal. And we also recognize our dependence on God as our ally, our strength, our shield (Psalm 28:7).

As parents, we're tempted to shield our children from every strife. The bully. The bad teacher. The pain of false accusations and unfair decisions and attacks on their faith. We want to protect them when we really should be teaching them how to protect themselves—to truly utilize the weapons of God's Word, prayer, truth, righteousness, peace, faith, and salvation. Are we helping them commit Scripture to heart? If so, God can bring those verses to mind, helping them respond to the enemy's strike. Are we teaching them to rely on prayer as an honest conversation that often results in answers? Then they'll know to seek his direction as they discern truth from lies and fight injustice. Are we teaching them how to settle into God's own peace in the midst of the most fearsome storm? If so, they'll be able to stand strong, even when confronting difficult circumstances.

If we want our kids to be battle-ready, we need to help them train with the weapons God has given us. Medieval knights didn't just slap on armor and enter the fray. Many were sent as children to serve as squires for full-fledged knights. They learned from a tender age how to wield the weight of a heavy sword, when to lift the shield, how to tend to wounds, and to utilize strategy. Can't you just see the little boys gathered around to watch the knights practice? Serving them as they prepared to go out, clean and whole? And then again when they came home bruised, bloody, and weary?

I think we'd do well, as parents, to consider ourselves knights, and our children squires, learning how to go to battle and return victorious. Too often we hide our struggles from our children. Kids need to know that skirmishes and strife are a part of life—just as much as they need to know that God has given us the means to prevail in those battles. They need to know we are far from defenseless. And that when we cry out to God in our weakest moments, he has the opportunity to do the most.

Rise, warrior, he breathes in our ears. And on trembling legs, we do so. We face the barrage again—the bad news from the doctor, the lawyer, the accountant. Or for kids, the bullying neighbor or the mean teacher. *Stand, warrior,* he whispers. *You shall stand.* And, drawing from deep within, we comprehend that he's given us every ounce of strength to do as he bids. To square our shoulders, lift our chins, and strap on the breastplate of righteousness, the shield of faith, the helmet of salvation, while raising the sword of the Spirit in our hand.

It's in the battle we are defined. When we know at last, who—and Whose—we really are.

Lord of every battle, I know that you see all. I know you allow me to struggle in order to build my battle muscles. I want to serve you better, standing strong with unmitigated trust and faith—and teach my child how to do the same. Forgive my fear. My cowardice. Forgive me for running rather than facing the battle at hand and trusting that you'll stand beside me. I am a grasshopper in my own eyes. Let me rise and be your warrior child, filled with confidence born of your Spirit. And help me lead my children by example, teaching them that you are our greatest ally. Amen.

Making It Personal

Are you in a battle now? Are you running, or are you standing with the confidence of a child loved by your heavenly Father? Why or why not?

_____

_____

_____

_____

_____

_____

_____

_____

_____

Making It Relevant

For younger children: Is it better to fight a bully or run away? How do you deal with kids who push you around?

For older children: What do you believe is worth fighting for? What would you be willing to sacrifice to protect it?

Day 9

I pray you'll experience unanswered prayers—and develop deeper, wider trust.

Do not be anxious about anything, but in everything, by prayer and petition, with thanksgiving, present your requests to God.

—Philippians 4:6

I'm terrible at waiting for anything I want. Almost as bad as my kids. Instant gratification? *I'm all about that.* Expedited shipping? *Sounds good.* Take it home today? *Please.*

I like streaming movies. Downloading books to my Kindle. Texting. Fast food.

More, more, more. Faster, faster, faster.

So when I have to wait, I find it incredibly frustrating. Especially when it comes to prayer. *Why, Lord, why?* I rail at the heavens. *Why do you not answer? When you KNOW how much I need to hear from you?* I wonder if he hasn't heard me. Or if he didn't quite grasp the depth of my longing. I question whether he's paying attention. Why he doesn't feel my visceral, raw *need.*

Eventually, I wonder if he's trying to teach me something. If I need to course-correct to get things in order. In other words, I start trying to figure out how to Get What I Want.

Or maybe it's patience he wants me to develop?

Sigh. Patience.

Or to wait upon his timing?

Sigh. Right. *His* timing.

It reminds me of the kids eagerly eying their Christmas gifts. Needling us, trying to finagle the parental nod to open an early present. "Just one," they plead. "Just *one.*" That's how I plead with God. "Just a hint, Lord. A tiny sign. A whisper. A nudge. *Please! C'mon!*"

Why do we make our kids wait? Why not give in, allow them to do as they ask? In my family, it's because Tim and I want to make the day special. Because the timing will be right. And because anticipation results in fuller appreciation of the gift. Even beyond Christmas, when it comes to many of their other requests, we require them to wait because they're asking for something they're simply not ready to receive. We know that the longed-for item or experience will be better, more suitable, more *right,* in a year, or two, or ten.

Could those things also be true when it comes to answered prayer?

I need to share with my kids both the power of prayer and the power of sold-out faith in the God who sees but is sometimes silent in his response, insisting that we wait. They need to know that some prayers go unanswered for years. Decades. Even generations. But that doesn't mean God is absent.

Because in the end, we see. Oh, we *see.* If not here, we will understand in heaven. How a quicker answer might have changed things—but not for the better. How if he'd granted that desire, we would have settled for so much less than what he had promised. How, if he'd spoken earlier, we wouldn't have leaned ever so much closer to him, listening, listening, listening. The gift of time allows us such perspective, doesn't it?

Paul says, "Do not be anxious about anything" and urges us to present our requests "with thanksgiving" (Philippians 4:6). He's not describing fretful, hand-wringing believers. He's describing how we all aspire to be in the waiting: Hopeful. Expectant. Trusting. Praise-filled. Such attitudes will come more easily to those whose hearts and minds are guarded by the peace of God (verse 7). And isn't that what we want for our children, as well as ourselves?

*God of Time, forgive my impatience. Help
me to learn that you hold the day, the month,
the year, and even the decade in your hand.
I know you transcend time. Help me and my
child to lean into you and claim our trust—
complete and utter trust—over our impatience. When you are silent, help us to wait
in peace, knowing you will answer, when and
how it is right. Help us to rest in your total
love for us, your desire that we be all that we
were born to be, as your sons and daughters.
Amen.*

MAKING IT PERSONAL

When did you last encounter the silence of God? Describe
your response when you felt he wasn't answering your prayers.

_____

_____

_____

_____

_____

_____

MAKING IT RELEVANT

For younger children: Why is it so hard to wait for something we want?

For older children: Why do you think God makes us wait for some things? What can we do while we wait?

Day 10

I pray you'll feel foolish—and know that the wise obey God anyway.

For the message of the cross is foolishness to those who are perishing, but to us who are being saved it is the power of God.

—1 Corinthians 1:18

My second grader doesn't like to be embarrassed. Nothing makes him angrier or hurts his feelings more than to suspect that someone is laughing at him. And my middle schooler and high schooler? Public embarrassment is enough to torpedo their whole week.

I think most of us prefer to protect our dignity. So how do we respond when serving Christ might cause damage to our image or our reputation?

Being a Christian writer allows me to serve God in a way that others admire. Most of the time it's clean and easy, especially when I'm writing to a Christian audience. But as I venture outward, attempting to be salt and light in a peppery, dark world, I find myself wrestling more with my word choices. Crafting carefully my posts on Twitter and Facebook to avoid anything that might tag me as one of "those closed-minded Christians." I constantly walk a thin line, not wanting to mess up my reach as I preach. And yet I don't want to be wimpy in expressing my faith. Back and forth I go.

And it's not just in my writing life that I worry about the impression I'm giving. I tend to chew over the things I've said in any situation, how I came across to others, the way I responded, for days afterward. (Clearly, long after everyone else has forgotten the event!) Why? Because I'm fretting over how it *appeared*. How others *perceived* me. And while I often tell my kids to shake off the perceptions of others and focus on how God sees them, I mostly fail to live it out myself.

If you could see me right now, you'd see me visually shaking myself. "What's with you, Lisa? Good grief! Have you learned nothing? *Nothing?* This life isn't about you. It's about Jesus. JESUS. And if you're not willing to do anything he asks—regardless of any damage it does to your image—what are you truly offering your God?"

The theologians call this *pride,* and they say every aspect of sin involves a measure of pride. It boils down to the "I." Greed says, *I deserve it.* Gluttony says, *I deserve a lot.* Lust declares, *I deserve you.* Anger announces, *I deserve it now and in this way!* Envy argues, *I deserve it more than you.* Laziness claims, *I deserve it without effort.*

So if Pride lurks at the root of every sin, insisting that it's all about us, how we're perceived and what we deserve, what's the polar opposite of it? Sold-out foolishness. Foolish generosity to combat greed; foolish, regimented attention to what we acquire in order to combat gluttony; foolish focus on our marriage—or our single hearts—to combat lust; foolish grace with others to combat anger; foolish love for others to combat envy; and freely given, foolish effort to accomplish goals we wish to meet.

I know. I *know.* It might make our friends shake their heads at us. *Why do you let them walk all over you? Why do you give so much? Why do you work so hard?* Feeling foolish makes us burn. None of us likes to feel less-than. Beneath. Lower.

Frankly, I even worry that the way I come across will have a negative effect on how others view Jesus. *Heavy sigh.* Yeah, that'd be pride again. Nothing can prevent Christ's purposes from being accomplished, even the mighty Me.

As a parent, I'm attempting to convey this lesson to our

kids: The earlier I submit, truly submit, and proclaim that he is God of All, the sooner he can use me, even when I am less than perfect. Even when it might appear foolish to others. And he can do the same with them. If they refuse to go to the movie that glorifies evil or sin, even though "everyone else" is, maybe "everyone else" will think twice about what they're watching or choose a different film. When they reach out to the uncool kid when no one else will, perhaps a suicide might be averted. If they dare to offer to pray for a hurting friend who looks down on Christians, maybe that friend will begin to seek God.

This life of discipleship is about embodying Jesus, regardless of the cost. Even if we have to sacrifice, trust, take a stand when nobody else agrees with us. Even if we have to step out into territory that others warn us against, because God is clearly leading us there. Even if we look like idiots because we only have our eyes on him.

> *God of the Universe, you humbled yourself to become man, so that I could be with you forever. You struggled, you suffered, you persevered, when all you had to do was speak and everything would change. You took on the nature of a servant so that you might know our struggle. Help me to teach my children to set aside pride and be willing to give their all—everything in them and in their life—*

> *for your cause. You are our Beginning and End. Everything in the middle is just a passing breath. Give us your perspective, Lord, and help us to bear the blows to our pride with character-building honor. Amen.*

MAKING IT PERSONAL

What was the hardest, most embarrassing thing you ever had to get through? What did you learn about yourself in the process?

_____

_____

_____

_____

_____

_____

_____

MAKING IT RELEVANT

For younger children: Why do you think it hurts when others think they're better than you are?

For older children: Do you think some people laughed at Jesus? Why do you think he allowed that?

Day 11

I pray you'll know what it is to be lonely—and find intimacy with the One who is always beside you.

I am with you and will watch over you wherever you go, and I will bring you back to this land. I will not leave you until I have done what I have promised you.

—Genesis 28:15

We sometimes fill our lives and social schedules with anyone who is available rather than with the people who will make our lives richer and more meaningful. We resist solitude because we perceive it as loneliness. And we don't only fill our lives with people who keep us in stasis—we also fill it with busy schedules, activities, responsibilities that keep us rolling from morning until night. Never pausing. Never giving us opportunity to feel the silence.

I've traveled by myself a few times for research. And I've discovered that nothing makes me feel more lonely than being in a foreign city, not speaking the language, not knowing exactly where everything is, not being able to decipher a menu or currency, nor having a working phone or Internet connection. Each time I've done it, it's forced me to such a place of vulnerability and isolation that I find myself in almost constant prayer. For protection. For peace. For guidance. For pleasure, even in the midst of experiencing something so amazing all alone. And I've glimpsed what monks and hermits knew well—that loneliness nurtures a dependency on and intimacy with God.

Now as parents, it breaks our hearts to see our kids lonely. To struggle in finding friends. To watch as party invitations are passed out but no envelopes are distributed in their direction. We ache when friends choose others over our children. But those seasons of loneliness can be precious instances when they begin to discover how God can stand in the gap for them and be the Friend who never leaves their side. And growing stronger in that knowledge will serve them when they must stand against the crowd for the right cause, even if it means they stand alone.

We need occasional jolts of loneliness—that separation from everything we've come to know and grown comfortable with—in order to look to our Savior anew. Sometimes that moment of feeling like no one understands us, no one believes in us, no one is taking our side, drives us to a new means of connecting with the One who always understands, always believes, always has faith in us.

Intimacy demands connection and communication. And that requires some effort. But how can we cultivate intimacy with God if we fill our hours doing everything we can to avoid it? Too often, we opt for the easier, the less-than, and then wonder why we do not end up feeling fulfilled, connected, bonded. Used wisely, the lonely times can draw us closer to our God than ever.

If we let *him* fill the empty spot, rather than cramming it with less-than stand-ins.

Constant Companion, you understand me when no one else does. Thank you for always being present for me and my children when we need you. Forgive us for buying the lie that we need other things and other people more than we need you. I want a strong and vibrant relationship with you, Lord. And I want that same thing for my child, more than anything. Help us each to seek you out consistently, not just when we're feeling lost and lonely. But redeem our lonely times, too, with a renewed intimacy with you. Amen.

MAKING IT PERSONAL

When did you feel the loneliest? How did God sustain you or draw near?

_____

_____

_____

_____

_____

_____

_____

_____

MAKING IT RELEVANT

For younger children: Have you ever been lonely? How do you see God around you?

For older children: What do you like or not like about being alone? How do you know that God will never leave you or forsake you?

Day 12

I pray you'll suffer loss—and witness how your Creator can use all things for good.

And we know that in all things God works for the good of those who love him, who have been called according to his purpose.

—Romans 8:28

L oss is a bloody, ruthless business. The anchoring point of a home, cut off via foreclosure. The stability of a job, shaken by a layoff. The partnership of a marriage, disintegrating into divorce. A friendship, sucked away by misunderstanding and miscommunication. A body, ravaged by disease. Worse…a life, extinguished.

We live in a fallen, sinful, imperfect world, and loss will eventually visit us all. The kind of suffering that makes our legs tremble so much we fall into a chair. Or to our knees. The kind of loss that literally steals our breath, that turns our heartbeat into something foreign, distant. It comes to each of us, in time. Regardless of the preventive measures we take, regardless of economic status or spiritual maturity, loss arrives. Are we prepared? Have we prepared our children?

When my niece was six years old, she died unexpectedly. Mady was a hard-won baby, an only child. And one bleak, black night, an undiagnosed heart condition sent her home to heaven. When the call came, it was an on-my-knees-on-the-kitchen-floor kind of moment. Later, I could only pray, *Why, Lord? Why this one? Why didn't you protect her? Why didn't you save her? How could you, Lord? How could you? Where were you?*

I was furious. I was heartbroken. I was lost inside the loss. And I knew I'd have to shepherd my kids through the midst of that pain, which made it all the harder. I talked to a counselor friend, desperately asking, "How on earth do I break this news to my little kids?"

She said, "You have to say over and over again: 'This is awful. This hurts. But it will be okay. I promise, in time, even though we'll always miss Mady, life will feel okay again.'" She reiterated that the key was to recognize the pain *but to also focus on the promise.* To cope, my kids had to know that it was okay to feel the agony, but they also needed to cling to hope.

Such experiences make our hearts bleed, make us question whether God still sits on his throne. And at that point, we choose to either remain angry at the God who appears absent or to trust in the God who is sovereign and continually present—regardless of how it *feels.*

As parents, we want to give our children—and ourselves—context when loss strikes, don't we? We try to help them see that a friend's move to another school opens their hearts to other, perhaps even better, friendships. We strive to showcase how a parent's job loss is an opportunity to differentiate what we want from what we need. We try to bolster them through physical loss and injury by encouraging them to invest more in their spiritual life. Context—trying to make sense of how God is using a step back to propel us forward—helps us sort things out in our heads and hearts and eases the pain.

But sometimes loss is inexplicable. We cannot see how God intends to use it for good. The answer might be a generation—or ten—away. Or we may not see the "why" this side of heaven. The question remains, will we trust in him even when we can't see the context? Proclaim our faith even through the agony? Pray, "I don't understand, Lord. I just don't understand. But I know you love me. Help me to rest in that and trust you to make this right in *your* time."

In the midst of the pain, in the hollow, widening ache, God reaches out to us and holds us and whispers, *I AM here. Regardless of how it feels. How it appears. And you can rest in my love. Trust me, no matter what happens.* And if we let him—if we let our children feel the weight of their loss without trying to explain it away—he can use our trust in him for his good purposes, even as we grieve.

Lord of All, I confess I hold tightly to the things I love, the things I declare mine. And when they are lost, it hurts. Help me to understand that you gave everything you had— your very Son—so that I might have an eternal relationship with you. Help me to teach my child that you see far beyond what we can, and that you use all things to bring us closer to you—even when those losses seem beyond comprehension. Help us to trust you through it all, Lord, even when we doubt. Amen.

MAKING IT PERSONAL

What loss are you still grieving, still searching to see how God will use it for good?

_____

_____

_____

_____

_____

_____

_____

_____

_____

MAKING IT RELEVANT

For younger children: How does God comfort us when we're sad?

For older children: Why do you think God allows good people to suffer and struggle?

I pray you'll be shattered—
and allow God to build you
up again.

I know that my Redeemer lives,
      and that in the end he will stand on
         the earth.
And after my skin has been destroyed,
      yet in my flesh I will see God…
      How my heart yearns within me!

—Job 19:25–27

Have you ever watched your child work on a school project and at some point recognize that he'd be best served by dismantling it all and starting fresh, applying what he'd learned? No one likes to do it. It hurts to take apart what we've put so much effort into—and we dwell on the lost hours, the lost supplies, the lost investment. But doesn't it often work out so much better if you start over from the ground up, free from the confines of a process gone bad?

I hold on to so much about myself and my life, focused on building myself up—regardless of how shoddy the foundation is—that it seems God often has to literally break me apart so that he can rebuild me properly. So when shattering events occur—when I've lost loved ones, love, or even a solid sense of self—when I'm rattled into little more than a pile of bones on the carpet, my Creator has a rare shot at remolding me into something closer to his image.

Key to the rebuilding process is to understand we are nothing without him breathing life in us, moving in and through us, using us. How exhilarating to recognize that he has vision for us—oh, such vision!—as we allow him to give us *his* eyes instead of insisting we see through our own. Such words of wisdom for us, if we only listen for his quiet whisper rather than the buzz and shouting of the world! Such perspective, if we can only slip on the "mind of Christ" and understand our circumstances as he does!

And though we ache when we witness our child's distress, we can draw confidence in knowing that the One who first brought her to life will bring her to life again. That we can trust him to hold our child, to help her to her knees, and eventually to her feet, certain that the experience ultimately will make her stronger.

My thought is this: most of us appear like antique mirrors, with some of the silver flaking off, marring our reflection of our God. If we suffer a shattering of that imperfect surface, Christ can heal us, rebuild us, replacing marred and nonreflective pieces with brand-new, clear ones. While our mirror may bear cracks—evidence of the wounds we've suffered—in time, we'll see that the new pieces look more like Jesus and less like us.

And as time goes on and the glass becomes fused, we'll gaze into that shattered-now-rebuilt mirror and see less of ourselves, more of him. And others will see it too.

> *Lord, as hard as it is, I pray you will break my child, shatter him in order to free him of the pieces that keep him from being a clearer reflection of you. Help us all to remember that you are the Potter and we are the clay. There are times when we feel cracked and dried, when we believe it's impossible that you will ever coax us back into pliable, moldable, fixable clay at all. Wash us clean, Savior. Free us from our sins. And make our humble lives something that glorifies you, regardless of what it takes to get there. Amen.*

MAKING IT PERSONAL

Do you believe that God can take a shattering event and re-build a person stronger than before? Why or why not?

_____

_____

_____

_____

_____

_____

_____

_____

MAKING IT RELEVANT

For younger children: Have you ever had to totally start over on a project to get it right? What made it better the second time through?

For older children: Have you ever insisted on pushing through on a project when you knew it just wasn't right? How did you feel about the end result? In what ways is that a little like our lives at times?

Day 14

I pray you'll be nearsighted—focusing on the present.

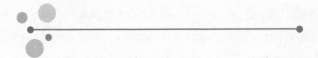

This is the day the LORD has made;
>   let us rejoice and be glad in it....
The LORD is God,
>   and he has made his light shine upon us.

—Psalm 118:24, 27

Our eyes are miracles in themselves. They process color and discern distance. They gather peripheral, as well as straight-on, visual information, sorting everything from the landscape passing by our car window to waves rolling onto the beach to ants crawling across the path.

We often watch multiple things at once. For example, just take a look at the evening national news. On screen, you'll likely see four different elements: the ticker stream listing big-stories-in-brief at the bottom; the subtle, waving design element behind the anchor; the anchor himself; and the story graphic on the top right. Our children have grown up viewing movies in 3-D and playing high-visual-impact games on the Wii or Xbox, as well as watching music videos and picture-in-picture television.

We've become accustomed to so much visual information and stimulation that our minds are set to operate at a frenetic pace. And when the visual stimuli slow, we grow a little restless, don't we? We're not content to play a board game when we can take part in an action game in 3-D on Nintendo. We prefer the high-octane, suspense movie to the more sedate PBS period piece with a lot of character development. We seek out the movie or the TV rather than sitting beneath a tree, watching the wind move among the leaves. I know, I know—I'm generalizing. You and your kids might be all about chess and classic books and the outdoors. But don't you sense a societal shift? A change that has all of us anticipating what's next, regardless of our preferences?

When we're constantly looking outward, beyond, to the

next thing, we often miss what's right before us. The moment. What God has for us right here, right now.

My kids get wrapped up in What's Next. The next family trip. The upcoming youth meeting. The test tomorrow. The finals. The newest episode of their favorite TV show. The next opportunity to beat their high score on the game. When they don't know what's coming, they get a little anxious. They want the future nailed down, understood, clear in their heads. They want to know the plan.

I get that. Because nobody loves The Plan like this mama loves The Plan. I revel in the anticipation, thinking through different scenarios, as well as feeling prepared. But sometimes I'm so forward-focused that I need Coke-bottle-thick glasses to see what's right before me. My kids are better at living in the present—fully embracing the moment. But as they age, I can see their focus shifting to what's-next rather than love-this-happening-right-now. Perhaps we lose our near-sight visual acuity as we age?

Psalm 119:105 tells us that God's Word is to be a lamp to our feet. The ancient author thought of a "lamp" as the flame from the wick of a small oil pot in his hand. Stand in a dark room with a lighted match, and you'll have an idea of what that meant—you can see little beyond an arm's reach, right?

That is how we are to live life with God. Looking at what he's illuminated, right before us. Not always anticipating what might be around the bend, over the next horizon, but focusing on *here, now.* To constantly be on the lookout for what's next is to miss the blessings at hand.

*God of Illumination, forgive me for being so
overstimulated and busy that I'm always looking ahead, around, rather than concentrating
on what you're bringing right before me. Help
me see you and your hand in my life. Help my
family live in and appreciate the moment.
Help us to recognize your gifts in the people
we meet, the activities of the day—everything
we can reach out and touch. And please help
my children to cling to The Moment rather
than obsessing about Tomorrow. Grant us
your sight, Lord. Make us aware of what you
want us to see, notice, and experience. Amen.*

MAKING IT PERSONAL

Pause now to focus on the blessings at your feet, right at this
moment, and take a moment to write them down.

_____

_____

_____

_____

_____

_____

MAKING IT RELEVANT

For younger children: What is something you appreciate, right now, that you can reach out and touch?

For older children: Is it hard for you to live life in "the moment" rather than always looking ahead? Why or why not?

Day 15

I pray you'll be farsighted—
able to see where our God is
leading us.

But thanks be to God, who always leads
us in triumphal procession in Christ
and through us spreads everywhere the
fragrance of the knowledge of him. For
we are to God the aroma of Christ among
those who are being saved and those who
are perishing.

—2 Corinthians 2:14–15

So we've talked about the importance of being aware of the blessings within the moment (Day 14). But there's a balance to this, for sure. Sometimes we get so distracted by the activities and events in our lives, the busyness and the momentary crises, that we forget to look beyond ourselves to our God, who gestures us forward or waves us back. We forget Who we're living for, and why we're walking this road at all. We're so focused on sight that we forget we *smell*—carrying the "aroma of Christ"—and that our aroma is either sweet or slightly stagnant, turned, like the old, forgotten perfume bottle in the back of the closet.

Even my prayers for my kids tend to focus on the pressures and demands of the moment, and I forget to pray that they might see the amazing, epic purposes of God unfolding before them and summoning them to be a part of his farsighted vision. The Trials of the Day absorb us all. The homework. The practice. The youth group meeting. How well somebody treated them (or didn't). How well they did on the test (or didn't). The praise or the hard word from Mom and Dad.

We parents get so lost in the demands of the day that we forget to teach our kids to keep their eyes on that horizon goal of becoming more like Christ, following his Father's lead. We become just as scattered and distracted as they are.

As believers in Christ, our key task in life is to make disciples of others (Matthew 28:19–20). If we look to the horizon, we'll see him there, beckoning us to go and make disciples, to baptize and teach others his ways. To *be* like Jesus to them, leading by example. We're also to invest in our relationship with the Savior, making it a priority to know him better. Inevitably, that will make our fragrance all the more attractive, and in time, others will come to us, wanting to know Jesus better too.

How do we translate that into our children's lives? We help them build a real and vibrant relationship with Jesus; find a solid mentor who challenges them to go deeper (because trust me, at some point, they'd rather hear it from someone besides us parents); teach them to live a life that others want "a piece of"—exuding a sweet attitude that draws others near; and encourage them to shut out the noise and busyness of life enough to slow down and focus on where God is leading.

If we understand that all of life is a "triumphal procession," life's priorities become clear. We move forward purposefully as God leads us on, seeking those who are hungry for life and sharing with them the Word that will satisfy their souls.

God of the Path, forgive me for getting so wrapped up in the distractions of daily life that I've lost sight of where you're leading me. Lift my chin. Help me focus on you and see how I can join you in what you are doing. Give my children a big-picture vision of your purposes and their role in your plan. Lead us on, Lord. Lead us on. Amen.

MAKING IT PERSONAL

Was the Great Commission (Matthew 28:19–20) meant for all of us? Do you believe God could use you to make disciples of others? What opportunities to do so has he placed in your life right now?

_____

_____

_____

_____

_____

_____

_____

_____

_____

MAKING IT RELEVANT

For younger children: How can you show others your faith in Jesus?

For older children: A lot of people think Christians "stink." Why do you think that is? How can we "smell good" to others, drawing them toward the faith, rather than driving them away?

Day **16**

I pray you'll lose a job—and
know that your Provider has
not forgotten you.

Consider the ravens: They do not sow or
reap, they have no storeroom or barn; yet
God feeds them. And how much more
valuable you are than birds!

—Luke 12:24

It's downright un-American to suggest celebrating a job loss. We've been raised on the premise that we pull ourselves up by the bootstraps when we're down. That if we work hard enough, try hard enough, we can accomplish anything. That nothing is out of reach for those willing to make the effort. It's the American Dream, right?

But sometimes God "gifts us" with the beauty of a pink slip. Whether we were a wrong fit for the job or among a group of people slated for layoff, we find ourselves suddenly wondering where the next rent or mortgage check will come from, how we'll put food on the table, or whether we should sign up the kiddos for soccer. We stare at the dwindling numbers in the checkbook and stack the bills in one bleak pile. Trips to the mall are suspended. Vacations are out of the question.

And the beauty is this: We can't find our way out. We can't fix it. We can look for the job, knock on every door possible, but if the God of All doesn't open one, we have to wait. And in the waiting, we get to see what he wants us to gain from this season—perhaps a winnowing of the frivolous, a better understanding of the difference between *want* and *need*, a renewed focus on trust and thankfulness, and even an opportunity to escape a dead-end job and move on to something bigger, better.

Right after college and newly engaged, I was desperate for a job and took the first thing that came up—a receptionist position in a busy dermatologist's office. Within two weeks I was fired because, as my supervisor observed, "Your heart isn't in it." I was devastated. I wept, alternately aghast and humiliated. If I couldn't hold down an entry-level job, how could I ever go after some of my long-term dreams in publishing? But being unemployed pushed me to consider where my Provider wanted to "feed me." And within six months I landed the Dream Entry-Level Job with—you guessed it—a *publisher*. And twenty years later, I look back in awe over a career in which I've been privileged to help launch hundreds and hundreds of books, including nearly forty with my own name on the cover.

What would have happened if I had been able to keep that receptionist job? I wanted it dearly. But God wanted something else for me.

I realize that you or your spouse may have lost a fulfilling job, perhaps even been forced out of a career. In our current economy, many have been searching months for the next thing, the way God wants to provide for them and their families. Dealing with the reality of unemployment is one of the more challenging elements of family life for parents to manage. We want our kids to feel secure, so our tendency is to pretend that everything is fine, even when they can feel that low-frequency radio wave in the air around the house that clearly reveals that everything is *not* fine.

How much better to bring them into the process, to teach them these things that we're learning as adults—thankfulness for how God provides day by day and trust that tomorrow rests safely in his hands? What if we raised our children to be utterly confident that their God will provide for them—

and not necessarily through the "perfect job"? Between getting fired and landing my first publishing job, I took temporary work at minimum wage. My parents housed and fed me. But all of that was *provision,* right? Our children need to know that God provides in different ways—sometimes through a paying job, and sometimes through family and friends and the Body, his church.

When we rely on God's strength rather than on our own skills, and when we accept whatever means he uses to "come through" for us, we can face setbacks and trials with confidence, trusting in him through it all.

Provider, being jobless scares me. I want you to use my abilities to your glory, but I also need enough to sustain my family—feed us, clothe us, shelter us. Help me to trust you, even when my very existence seems tenuous. Even if I have to let go of what I consider "mine" in order to accept what you have next for me. Help me to remember that you see me and that you are daily shaping me to look a little more like your Son. Help me to keep my eyes on you through that process. And when my children face joblessness themselves, teach them the same. Keep us focused on your strength and your promise to meet our needs, rather than trusting in our own skills. I thank you, Lord, and praise you for today's provision. Comfort my children with the knowledge that you will see to their needs too. Amen.

MAKING IT PERSONAL

Have you or your spouse ever been out of work and out of money? How did that, or would that, shape your faith in God and how he provides?

_____

_____

_____

_____

_____

_____

_____

_____

MAKING IT RELEVANT

For younger children: What is something you want from the store? What is something you need, every day?

For older children: What's the difference between what we want and what we need? Can you think of some examples?

Day 17

I pray you'll brush up against death—and catch a glimpse of eternity.

But our citizenship is in heaven. And we eagerly await a Savior from there, the Lord Jesus Christ, who, by the power that enables him to bring everything under his control, will transform our lowly bodies so that they will be like his glorious body.

—Philippians 3:20–21

We all know that kids think of themselves as invincible. And there's a gift in that—a freedom that allows them to venture farther, higher, wider than if they were born knowing, truly knowing, that their lives were finite. Think about it. Wouldn't you be more adventurous, risk a bit more if you didn't fear death yourself? If you hadn't brushed up against it or known others who had?

As parents, there's a part of us that wants to preserve the illusion, to focus on the bright light of life, skirting any shadows of death. We promise to be there "forever" for our children. We promise they'll "always" have us. But we can only do that by ignoring the fact that death comes to us all, and we're most certainly not here, *always* and *forever*.

It's natural to avoid the subject of death. We were created by the God of life, who loves life. But after the Fall, death became a part of our world, and each time we face it, we're reminded that we're far, far from Eden and how God hoped our world would be. Coming to terms with death inevitably brings us sorrow, a sliver of his own grief. But there's also joy in anticipating the far greater adventure ahead. Scripture tells us that our "lowly bodies" will be like Christ's in heaven. So much beauty lies ahead of us—no more illness, no more death, life eternal—but still we cling to what we know here, now.

Last week, my dear friend's son, a freshman in college, found out that his best friend and spiritual mentor, Ryan, had died in a climbing accident. I wept with my friend as she prepared to walk her son through the sorrow and shock, grieving with her and for the family who had lost such a faithful, incredible young man. The kids flew home from college from far and wide to celebrate his life, to remember, but also to contemplate the fact that he now awaits them in our forever home. Sarah described the memorial service as "a bit of heaven. Like you could reach out and touch it. Hear the angels sing."

Clearly it was one of those rare moments when the separation between heaven and earth thins, and we catch a glimpse of the hope and joy that await us all. And through that weekend of tears and laughter, celebration and heartrending sorrow, I believe each of those who mourned Ryan was given new gifts: appreciation for relationship with Christ, which assures us of our place in heaven; joy in the knowledge that one day all believers will be reunited; and awareness that our days on earth are few and we're to make the most of them.

To live with an awareness that our present reality is but a steppingstone to something greater infuses our present with depth and meaning, as well as context and hope. God loves us and has made a way for us to be with him forever (John 3:16), and through a relationship with Christ, we will live on in heaven (Acts 4:12). As much as we love our lives now, and value each day we are given, so much more awaits us. *So much!*

This is what I strive to teach my children: to live in joy for today balanced by hope for tomorrow. I want them to understand that God holds them when they grieve, weeps with them when they've lost someone dear, but he's pointing onward, to a time when all grief ends. That is the gift of death—the glimpse of the eternal, just around the corner.

Savior, thank you for conquering death so that we might live forever with you. Help me to trust, even when faced with loss and grief. Help me to know that you have not turned away, but are closer than ever, and your arms are around me. Give me the words to speak to my children about this hard subject. You know I'd rather ignore it. Help me lay a foundation of hope for them, so that when death visits, they can cling to the hope you've given us in eternal life. Amen.

Making It Personal

Did anyone close to you die when you were in your twenties or younger? Did you deal with it as you would now, later in life? How has your perspective on death changed as you've matured?

_____

_____

_____

_____

_____

_____

_____

MAKING IT RELEVANT

For younger children: What do you think heaven will be like?

For older children: Do you ever think about heaven? Who will you be most excited to see again? What do you think Jesus will say to you?

Day 18

I pray you'll have to wait—and learn the value of patience.

We know that the whole creation has been groaning as in the pains of childbirth right up to the present time.... For in this hope we were saved. But hope that is seen is no hope at all. Who hopes for what he already has? But if we hope for what we do not yet have, we wait for it patiently.

—Romans 8:22, 24–25

I've been writing books for about twenty years. When I first started out, I longed for all the markers of success. A dedicated readership. Fans. Sales. Bestsellers. I looked at other writers, and I wanted what they had, ignoring the fact that they'd been at it for a long, long time. I didn't like thinking about how they'd worked at the craft. Figured out winning proposals to garner contracts. Cultivated and fostered readership. I just wanted that Finish Line moment, the triumphant crossing, hands raised, crowds roaring. The rush of victory.

Yeah, I'm lazy and demanding like that. I'm not proud of it. And it wasn't just my writing career that made me crazy with the waiting. I've also resented the delays that came with finding a husband. Landing a job. Securing another publishing contract. Getting pregnant. Taking off on a dream vacation.

And there are some things that I'm so glad I *didn't* get, back when I was longing with all my heart for them. Wanting, wishing, wailing to God to make the ex-boyfriend return to me, on his knees, hands clasped before him to beg my forgiveness. Had he done so, I might never have met the man who is a much better match for me—my husband. Or chasing the entry-level job that I thought I wanted in one industry, one that would've kept me from discovering my abilities in another. In fact, if I'd landed that position, I might not have written this book (or any other, for that matter). Time and distance give us perspective.

My kids have a hard time with waiting too. They're

racked with impatience to find out if they got the role or if they get to play a certain position on the team. They complain about how long it's taking to save enough money for the coveted item. Or go on a trip with a friend. Or make the grade. All of these desires burn hot, hot, hot at that moment. But the week after it's been resolved one way or another? The urgency has cooled, even been forgotten, for the most part.

Some of our waiting is much more intense. More intimate and tender. We wait to see if a person might be the heart-friend we're longing for. We check our phone, wondering if the doctor has left us news about our test results. We search our soul, longing for the depression or grief to lift. We bear through physical pain, suffering, hoping we've not been forgotten.

But in the waiting we are forced out of ourselves. Out of our own intentions and our own capacity to make the world behave as we believe it should. That's why I'm convinced we don't do our children any favors by providing a quick resolution to whatever they're waiting for. Their agitation weighs heavily on us because it awakens our own frustration and lack of patience. But in the waiting, we all come to grips with the fact that we are not in control. We're compelled to trust the God who rules. We rediscover the value of patience and why it's listed as one of the gifts of the Spirit, along with such things as love, joy, and peace (Galatians 5:22–23).

And gradually, if we let them wait, our children learn those things too. They discover for themselves what it means to let go and rest in faith. To accept that God is far bigger than we are and that the desires of their hearts will arrive if and when he deems it right. They start to lean on the truth that God's plans, bigger and better, are constantly unfolding. And that we are not forgotten, no matter how it hurts to wait.

Just writing those words makes me take a deep breath and remember that I am small and my God is big. I remember he sees me, and knows me, and loves me, as he does my children. And if I love him in return, I can wait, confident and at peace, for what may come, for *all* of us—trusting him with what *is* rather than what *might be*.

Lord of All, you see me. You see inside me. You know all that I long for, hunger for. Sometimes it's almost harder watching my children wait for something than it is to be "on hold" myself. Help me to have the strength to allow patience to develop in them, knowing it will serve them in a much greater way than if I "rescue" them or resolve it myself. Help each of us to embrace this waiting business. You know we're not good at it. Thank you for the reminder that you are God, that you are in control, and we are not. Help us to rest in that rather than resist it. Amen.

MAKING IT PERSONAL

What's the hardest thing you've ever had to wait for? Looking back, what did you gain by waiting?

_____

_____

_____

_____

_____

_____

_____

_____

_____

MAKING IT RELEVANT

For younger children: Do you think you appreciate a gift more if you get it right away, or when you've waited and waited and waited for it, and then get it, like at Christmas?

For older children: Can you think of a time when God left you waiting for something you thought you wanted, and you were later glad you didn't get it right away?

Day 19

I pray you'll have selective hearing—deaf to all but the Father's voice.

I am the good shepherd; I know my sheep
and my sheep know me—just as the
Father knows me and I know the Father—
and I lay down my life for the sheep....
They...will listen to my voice, and there
shall be one flock and one shepherd.

—John 10:14–16

W e live in a noisy world. Years ago, TV and radio options were limited. If we didn't like what was on, we turned it off. Not so anymore. Cable offers an endless supply of shows, and if you don't find what you want there, you certainly can on the Internet. Same with radio—now you can stream music and only hear your favorites. We have 24-hour news, 24-hour weather, 24-hour politics, 24-hour sports, 24-hour cooking shows. Every which way you look, there's more than enough to fill your ears and mind.

It's overwhelming, really. But most of us have a hard time shutting it off. I'll battle sleep, wanting to see the end of this show...and then getting caught up in the next one. I'm reluctant to let the room fill with silence. *Because I might be missing something.*

Invariably, we *are* missing something. Often, it's God's voice.

And this isn't an adults-only problem. How do we teach our kids how to listen to their Father's still, small voice when texts and Facebook and Twitter and whatever's new on the Net take up their every waking moment? It doesn't have to be *audible* to be *loud*. Even we parents attempt to take the place of the Holy Spirit for our children at times, listening and interpreting for them about "God's direction" and "what he wants you to do," becoming a part of the noise in their ears.

Learning to wait quietly to hear from God is not a natural or easy thing. Oh, how I long for it to be simple and obvious! But our children learned to communicate—to form words and use different tones—from us, their parents. If we are not modeling how to listen—and telling our kids how God speaks to us—how will they learn to hear from him too? Perhaps we need to do more modeling and less interpreting, so they can begin the process of developing their own listening skills to hear the Shepherd's voice.

Sometimes I walk with my iPod buds in my ears, but instead of music or a podcast, I elect to listen to nothing at all because my brain is already noisy enough. I want to think through something big, or a hundred small things. And I want to pray—and have the bandwidth to hear from my God. I don't want to have to face an emergency in order to seek him out, to remember how to communicate with him. I want to be in such constant communication that we truly become one. So that I can serve him well, with his strength flowing through me and his voice guiding me.

In the same way, we need to teach our children to filter out his voice from the noise of their lives. That may involve allowing them to get overwhelmed and overbusy and overloaded so they can experience the relief that comes when they finally slow down. It may require us to help them make good scheduling choices so their lives aren't so noisy. Or best of all, we might encourage them to seek out God's direction when they need advice rather than filling the airwaves with our own voices.

If we are to be his hands and feet, we have to be able to hear him. Feel that tug, that nudge, that shove—to act…or speak…or step aside…or be still—and do what he's asked us to do, right then. We want to be deaf to all but his whisper in our ears.

*Lord, you call to me, and too often I can't
answer because I am deafened by the world.
I've chosen noise over you. Distractions. Idle
interests. If I choose anything over you, I
know it's an idol of sorts, and I confess that
entertainment has become an idol to me at
times. I want to hear you, Father. I want to
make time for you, first. I want to be in constant communication with you, feeling your
joy, your pain. Obeying your will. Make me
deaf to anything other than you, first. Amen.*

MAKING IT PERSONAL

Describe an occasion when God's whisper to you became a
shout—one that really shook you—in order to get your
attention.

_____

_____

_____

_____

_____

_____

_____

MAKING IT RELEVANT

For younger children: If you could hear God, like you hear me right now, what do you think he would say to you?

For older children: Have you ever heard God speak in your heart? If so, what was he trying to tell you? And if not, how can you be in the right space—physically, mentally, spiritually—in order to hear from him?

Day 20

I pray you'll know fear—and find courage in living with God beside you.

What, then, shall we say in response to this? If God is for us, who can be against us? He who did not spare his own Son, but gave him up for us all—how will he not also, along with him, graciously give us all things?

—Romans 8:31–32

I adore that Scripture: *If God is for us, who can be against us?* It's so brave and full of glory, isn't it? But the voices in my head go something like this:

> "If God is for us, who can be against us?"
> (Beats chest.) "Yeah!"
> *Well, actually, a lot can be against you.*
> "Like who? What?"
> *Like Satan, for one. You know, the Dark Side.*
> *The enemy.*
> "But God is Lord of all. Satan fights him,
> but God is the ultimate victor."
> *True. But it can hurt a lot before the end. Look at Job.*
> "Oh. Yeah."

Fear. It overwhelms all of us at times.

But that's not always a bad thing.

I've been in fear for my life a few times. In a riptide in Hawaii, which very nearly drowned me. When a robber held a gun to my head. On a snow-packed Wyoming road with eighty-mile-per-hour winds. But those are just my big, dramatic moments.

I've also struggled with ongoing, niggling fears, the kind that eat away at my peace for days or weeks or years. *What if I can't meet my bills? What if the company goes bankrupt? What if this illness is something more? What if this minor thing becomes a future disability? What if the car dies? What if the house floods?*

My children fear other things. *What if I fail that test? What if they make fun of me? What if I don't get asked to the dance? What if everyone gets invited to the party but me? What if nobody talks to me?* And to all those we can add the many fears we parents carry on their behalf—for their safety, their health, their future.

Too often we get lost in the what-ifs instead of walking with our God through the what-is. We try to usurp his role by enhancing our sense of security: a new burglar alarm; a bigger paycheck; a car with better airbags. Yet again we find ourselves grabbing for control when, ultimately, we have none.

In our times of fear, and even in our times of bravery, he wants us to slip our hands into his and whisper (or scream), *Be with me, God. I know you're with me! Help me through this.* He wants fear to serve as a reminder that we find our strength in him. In times of distress, we are to draw closer to him and face our fears, knowing the Lion of Judah is by our side. The only thing we are to fear is God himself. Not illness. Not loss. Not bankruptcy. Not joblessness. Not being alone. Not... [you fill in the blank].

Sometimes God chooses to spare us or deliver us from our problems. Sometimes he does not. But always, always he is by our side. Think about your children. Undoubtedly, you'd like to fix their problems. Make bumpy roads smooth. But sometimes we simply have to ride beside them over those rough patches, encouraging them onward. We're to teach them to stare their fears straight in the eye and answer their worst what-ifs with, "And so? What if it *does* happen?"

Regardless of what life brings—be they rivers that threaten to drown us or fires that might burn us—our God walks beside us (Isaiah 43:2). And if we were created by him and for him to be with him, ultimately, that's where we have to rest. There, in that sweet spot, fear is absent, courage fills us, and peace rules.

Mighty God, I confess I want to rule my own life. I look to other things besides you to bring me comfort and security. Help me open my clenched hands and release to you whatever or whomever I fear I may lose. Help me place my very life in your hands. My children's lives. Trusting you without fail. And help me to teach my child how to trust you too, even when life is scary. Make us courageous, brave warriors, Lord, knowing you are with us through it all. Amen.

MAKING IT PERSONAL

What do you fear most, right now? What if it came to pass? How do you think God might step in, before, during or afterward?

_____

_____

_____

MAKING IT RELEVANT

For younger children: What is one thing that scares you? Do you know that God is beside you all the time?

For older children: What's the biggest fear in your life right now? How do you think God wants you to deal with that?

Day 21

I pray you'll take crazy risks—
and dare to adventure where
your Shepherd leads.

As Jesus was walking beside the Sea of
Galilee, he saw two brothers, Simon called
Peter and his brother Andrew. They were
casting a net into the lake, for they were
fishermen. "Come, follow me," Jesus said,
"and I will make you fishers of men."

—Matthew 4:18–19

As children or young adults, we tended to venture out of our circle of the known, exploring, experimenting, excited to discover what life offered. Willing to gamble that whatever we found would be worth the risk. Sure, we fell down, we got hurt. But then we brushed ourselves off and tried not to make the same mistakes again. But that's the rub: at some point, most of us started avoiding risks out of fear of making mistakes.

Certainly, as we grow older, risks become less and less appealing. And even the more adventurous among us give greater thought to potential risks before we leap into adventure.

The danger then is that we'll begin to view *all* future risks more in terms of potential mistakes than as possible boons. And gradually, this keeps us from venturing out of what becomes an ever-shrinking circle.

But here's the thing: God calls us into *ever-widening* circles. If our "known world" isn't expanding every year, we are stagnating, or even retreating. Our God doesn't call us to hunker down and stay safe. He calls us to follow where he leads and to trust him to see us through whatever results.

What if James and John, or Peter and Andrew, hadn't dropped their nets and followed where Jesus led? Talk about a crazy risk. They walked away from family, the family business, their hometown—everyone they knew and loved—to follow an out-of-work carpenter in threadbare sandals and listen to him preach. Can you imagine their "what are you doing with your life?" conversation with Mom and Dad?

But consider what they would've missed had they turned

down the Shepherd's call! Life would have been comfortable and conventional, sure. But it would've been dreary and dull compared to the incredible experiences Jesus introduced them to. Covenant relationship. A bond—mental, emotional, spiritual, physical—with the Holy One. And the power of his kingdom, loosed on earth, through their hands and speech and prayer. Just think how unsettling it all must have been. Struggling to make sense of Jesus's death, resurrection, and ascension. Shocked that the Christ was giving them the training to carry on his good work. Scared that they'd never be able to represent him well. And eventually amazed, as they saw the good news begin to spread across the world.

As parents, we have to be daring. We're called to model faithful risk-taking, sharing with our children when we think God is leading us into something that scares us but which we know we must do in order to live as faithful followers. And we also have to carefully avoid the temptation to shield our children from risk—the impulse to talk them out of taking the mission trip, or participating in inner-city outreach, or even chasing the "impractical" career. If they feel led to do something because God has laid it on their hearts, and we want them to pursue brave, courageous, faithful discipleship—we must prayerfully cheer them on.

Shepherd, help me to answer your call with my chin up and my shoulders back. Help me to be brave, courageous. Teach me to

> *distinguish wisdom from fear and to carefully
> set fear aside, knowing that the evil one likes
> to use it as a weapon. Help me to fear only
> the risk of not doing as you have willed. And
> make my child a risk-taker, an adventure-
> seeker after the biggest adrenaline rush of all:
> your kingdom action. Infuse her with your
> wisdom to discern when to exercise caution
> and when to abandon it, all the while trust-
> ing in you. Use us all as your servants, Lord.
> Lead us. We are yours. Amen.*

MAKING IT PERSONAL

What's the biggest risk you ever took that didn't work out, in the world's eyes? Looking back, what did you gain or how did you grow from that experience?

_____

_____

_____

_____

_____

_____

_____

_____

MAKING IT RELEVANT

For younger children: What's the scariest thing you've ever done? How did you feel after it was over?

For older children: What's the scariest thing God could ask you to do? Do you think he'd give you what you needed to see it through? Why or why not?

Day 22

I pray you'll face financial hardship—and see how God is after something bigger than food and shelter.

So do not worry, saying, "What shall we eat?" or "What shall we drink?" or "What shall we wear?" For the pagans run after all these things, and your heavenly Father knows that you need them. But seek first his kingdom and his righteousness, and all these things will be given to you as well.

—Matthew 6:31–33

My teen is desperate for a job. Not because she really wants to work, but because she wants spending money of her own. The ability to save for a car and then pay for gas. Go shopping for clothes. I'm eager for that too. I like the idea of her having those freedoms, but I also know it will help her appreciate just how much things cost. What it means to budget. To save up for something.

Becoming self-sufficient and taking care of yourself is part of growing up. But independence can be a dangerous thing to strive for. It puts us at risk of believing we can be masters of our destiny. God continues to use financial strife as a means of bringing me to my knees and reminding me I am *not* my own master. Ultimately, I believe he's after my submission.

When my husband and I have plenty, I don't look to God as often. I feel I'm on top of things. And when we stare at lean bank-account balances, guess which way I'm looking? Yep. Right at God. It's really no wonder that he continues to use this method of teaching me lessons about who is truly Lord of my life and why I should trust him.

The fact is, God never wanted us to become self-sufficient. He created the garden so that we would have everything we needed. After the Fall, we knew we would have to toil for food and shelter, but he never wanted us to cease looking to him as the Provider, the Sustainer.

For us today, it often takes a shattering of the dark glass—the myth of our "self-sufficiency"—to discover that our lives are more satisfying when we trust our Daddy to take care of us rather than constantly striving to meet our own needs.

Missionaries discover this, relying on support from others as well as from God. For the rest of us, the wallets and savings accounts often have to be empty before we look up in desperation. And then we find that somehow, miraculously, he takes care of us.

But why do we insist on perpetuating the myth that we can take care of ourselves? Why do we push our children to get into the best colleges, so they can get into the best careers, so they can bring home the best paycheck, so they can send their children to the best private schools, so our grandchildren can get into the best colleges…and so on, for generations? I'm not suggesting we give up on doing our best or working hard; we're to give our all in whatever we do (Colossians 3:23–24). But Jesus, in his Sermon on the Mount, tells us the *most* excellent thing is to seek after God's righteousness—his holiness, his purity, his aversion to sin—and to be his Body in the world, serving the kingdom. *After* that, "all these things"—all our physical needs—will be taken care of as well (Matthew 6:33).

All too often, we find ourselves chasing things in backward fashion. God will meet our most vital, primary needs. But first we must chase after what is most vital and primary to him. That's why financial hardship can turn out to be an answer to prayer for our kids—and for us.

Lord, you know I draw comfort from having money in the bank, but I never want it to be more of a shield than my faith is. You also

know I like to take care of myself, but that's really just pride talking. You are the One who takes care of me, and you have my best interests at heart. As my child faces adult realities, no matter what's in his wallet, help him to wholeheartedly serve you and your kingdom. Remind each of us to fully recognize that all blessings come from you. And help us honor your gifts every day. In Jesus's name, amen.

MAKING IT PERSONAL

What's the worst thing that would happen if you went broke? Can you see any blessings that might arise out of that hard experience? (Or maybe you've already experienced it or are even in the midst of it; if so, take note of every blessing you can identify.)

_____

_____

_____

_____

_____

_____

_____

MAKING IT RELEVANT

For younger children: How has God taken care of you today? What are some ways he has provided for you?

For older children: Why do you think God wants us to rely more on him than on ourselves?

Day 23

I pray you'll be disappointed in people—and realize that we're all fallible, sinful, and redeemable.

But he was pierced for our transgressions,
　　he was crushed for our iniquities;
the punishment that brought us peace was
　　upon him,
　　and by his wounds we are healed.
We all, like sheep, have gone astray,
　　each of us has turned to his own way;
and the LORD has laid on him
　　the iniquity of us all.

—Isaiah 53:5–6

There's nothing like working in a Christian industry to topple your belief that someone might be immune to sin. I was fresh out of college, newly rededicated to my faith, with stars in my eyes and working for The Cause of Christ, when I watched one Christian celebrity I admired confess to adultery and another to embezzlement. I discovered a Christian agent falsely representing his client. I watched my Christian boss manipulating others and putting himself before the company. All of which left me not only disillusioned but a little skeptical about whether anyone could truly be trusted to put God first.

Now my teen is discovering that people she's long respected and looked up to are only human after all. She's reached that point of maturity when the stars fade and reality washes over her, cold and clear, giving her new eyes to see people as they truly are.

So I'm hoping I can help her discover what I learned in those early years of my career. Yes, it's incredibly disappointing when someone we admire gives in to temptation. But those disillusioning revelations confirm three crucial truths: No matter how long we're on this road of faith, sin can still ensnare us; the more we do for the kingdom, the greater a target we become to the enemy; and God can use us, in spite of our sin, to accomplish his good work. All of us.

The trouble with building people up in our minds and hearts is that we forget that they're as human as we are. That said, I maintain we all need a mentor to lead us—and if that person is not someone who resists sin with everything in them and who is accountable to their own mentor, we need to find another. Because we always need a shepherd ahead of us, to encourage us to give our best to this discipleship thing, even as we lead our own sheep behind us.

With that order of accountability in place, we also need to treat our brothers and sisters with a hefty dose of grace, knowing that the enemy is on the prowl, and none of us are ever entirely free from sin, this side of paradise.

Oscar Wilde said, "Every saint has a past, and every sinner has a future."[1] I love that. When we recognize that all the "saints" we've placed on pedestals struggled to get to that place of honor—and likely struggle to maintain their virtue—and when we look at our fellow sinners with the view that they're saints in training, just like us…we begin to spend less time wallowing in disappointment and despair, and more time awash in God's love. Grace. Peace. Forgiveness. Hope. Vision.

And in doing so, we become just a little bit better at this saint business.

---

1. Oscar Wilde, *A Woman of No Importance,* Act 3.

God of Love, thank you for saving me from my sin. Help me to live as you want me to, avoiding sin and embodying love, joy, peace, patience, faithfulness, gentleness, kindness, and self-control. Give me the spiritual strength to mentally and physically turn away from the sin that calls to me most persuasively. Open my child's eyes to the imperfections in his heroes, so he remembers that only One is flawless. And help us all to move from "disappointment" over our fellow sinners' failures to an honest perspective, full of grace and love toward others. Encourage us to confess, get up, brush ourselves off, and try again to be more like you. Help us to forgive as we have been forgiven. Amen.

MAKING IT PERSONAL

What sin do you have to battle every day? How does that knowledge shape your attitude toward those who have disappointed you in failing to conquer their own sin?

_____

_____

_____

_____

_____

_____

_____

_____

MAKING IT RELEVANT

For younger children: What are you tempted to do that you know you're not supposed to do? What keeps you from doing it?

For older children: What sin do you find hardest to battle? How have you seen someone fall into sin and disappoint others? Is their sin any worse than our own?

Day 24

I pray your beliefs will be challenged—and the roots of your faith will be strengthened.

Therefore everyone who hears these words of mine and puts them into practice is like a wise man who built his house on the rock. The rain came down, the streams rose, and the winds blew and beat against that house; yet it did not fall, because it had its foundation on the rock.

—Matthew 7:24–25

College used to be the Great Time of Questioning. The time when faith came under fire and you were forced to account for what you believe. The timing seemed ideal, because you had a certain level of maturity and could tackle it as a blossoming adult. But these days, my high schooler and middle schooler are coming up against kids who describe themselves as dedicated atheists. And while, as my husband says, it takes a lot of faith to be an atheist, my children find themselves compelled to defend their beliefs. And that's a good thing.

It's good when we have to defend our beliefs, because it means we're both interfacing with nonbelievers and deciphering why we believe what we do. But far too frequently, when our faith has come under fire, believers circle the wagons rather than continuing into the frontier. We send our children to Christian schools. We socialize with other Christians. We only shop in Christian bookstores.

Certainly, we can draw strength and a solid foundation from Christian schools, Christian friends, Christian books. But then we are meant to move out into the world and speak of that strength and foundation to unbelievers.

It's fairly common for Christians when faced with the hard question, "Why do you believe what you do?" to answer with a shrug of the shoulders and the classic line, "It's a leap of faith; you just gotta believe." But to be effective witnesses, we have to bring more to the table than that. Christ calls us to go and disciple others, first and foremost (Matthew 28:19). He didn't say to build churches. He said to disciple others. And frankly, not very many people are won to a life of discipleship by someone shrugging and giving them The Leap Line. They're won over by sold-out disciples who've been transformed by their relationship with Jesus. They're won over by seeing life lived differently and feeling a tug within that says, *I want a piece of that. That love. That joy. That peace. That security.* They're won over by people who can listen to an opposing perspective without getting angry and upset, and then share their own perspective with humble confidence.

But as important as it is to teach our children to live out their faith, they also need to be able to explain it (1 Peter 3:15). Believe me, there are far more cogent defenders of the faith than I. But we all—including our kids—need to be ready to respond, and respond well, to questions about the basics of what we believe.

For me, the core truths begin with the fact that I believe we live in a world that was created, on purpose. Look to the intricacies of the eyeball or the elaborate interrelation of ecology, and most would agree a Creator was involved. Second, I believe that the Creator of this world wants a relationship with me. That I was created to be in relationship with him, and with others in order to lead them toward relationship with him. I believe I am a sinner and need forgiveness for my sin. And that God so loved me and my fellow brothers and sisters that he made the ultimate sacrifice, through his Son, Jesus, so that I might never be separated from him again.

Finally, I believe that, because I am in relationship with him, he uses me for his good purposes. And that relationship makes my life better, richer, fuller than it could possibly be without him.

Are my kids ready to say the same? We're working on it. Discipleship is a lifelong process, and coming to terms with the hard questions—and responding with satisfactory answers—is a big part of it.

> *Defender, I get scared when I'm faced with the brainiacs who attack the faith. I'm fearful I'll look foolish, and I'll fail you. Make us brave, Lord. Rather than insulating ourselves from those who challenge our faith, bring me and my child into contact with people who need to hear your truth. Speak through our demeanor and actions as well as through our words. May our very lives declare the power of faith and the power of you. Make it unmistakable in us, Lord. And keep us from stepping on our own toes. Help us rest in the simple, quiet word and the core truths, rather than worry about "winning" any debate.*
> *Amen.*

MAKING IT PERSONAL

Have you ever been asked why you believe what you believe?
Were you ready? Are you ready now?

_____

_____

_____

_____

_____

_____

_____

_____

_____

_____

MAKING IT RELEVANT

For younger children: How do you know God loves you?

For older children: Are you secure in your faith and the basics
of what you believe? What do you still need to get settled in
order to be ready to defend what you believe?

Day 25

I pray you'll be confronted by your shortcomings—and recognize you need a Savior.

Do not think of yourself more highly than you ought, but rather think of yourself with sober judgment, in accordance with the measure of faith God has given you.

—Romans 12:3

Y ou couldn't pay me to go back to middle school. Living through it again as a parent is excruciating enough. It brings back all the memories, all the insecurity. Vying for attention. Vying to be invisible. Trying to impress friends. Fighting with friends. Hoping for a boy's attention. Achieving social status. Making peace with an evolving body.

Round one with our eldest was tough enough. She's a tender soul, and everything hurt. And while middle school is a mean place for anyone, it was really tough on Liv. And now with my middlest, it's tough in a new way. Because she's scrappy. And prickly. Rather than dodging the fight, she takes 'em on, head-on. It's exhausting. She comes home on some days feeling that things went pretty well. On others she returns with a ledger of complaints. And it's all about those other kids. Their faults. Their sins. Their problems. Their issues. How they're making her life difficult.

The thing is, most counselors will tell you that if you're having trouble with everyone else, a good place to start is some self-examination. But it's much easier and far more comfortable to look at everyone else, right? I know I'd rather notice that woman's penchant for gossip and that man's wandering eye than acknowledge my own loose tongue or sinful fantasies. I'd rather consider that woman's obvious trouble with controlling her appetite than my own, continual weight problem. I find it easier to condemn his pride issues than to consider the more subtle ways the same sin is arising in my own life.

Really, in some ways, I'm still in middle school. Still struggling to make sure I measure up better than others, at least outwardly. Still wanting to be liked. Still wanting people to follow me, to look up to me. And as a parent, I tend to encourage my kids' middle-school mentality too—propping up their self-esteem, reassuring them they're just as good as (or even "better than") so-and-so, soothing their hurts without investing the energy to get to the core of the matter.

But as with anything, balance is the key, right? We're to help our kids build healthy self-esteem and yet also honestly confront the ways they need to improve their walk—chiefly by pointing them toward Christ.

Sin is the great equalizer. And if we own our shortcomings, if we recognize that our sins are no greater, no less than those of our brothers and sisters, we recognize we're on the same journey, with the same needs, and all in need of a Savior. All of us are striving to settle into a life of meaningful relationship with the only One who makes it all worthwhile: Jesus.

God does not call us to be worms, writhing on the ground in woe over our sins. But he does call us to be warriors, submitted to our King. Strong enough to bow in humility before him and confess what we've done wrong. Because in doing that, we invite him to help us do battle against those sins that threaten our hearts. And if we can demonstrate that humility in front of our children, freely admitting where we fail and striving to do better, they will do the same.

Savior, I'm as reluctant to own my sins as my children are. I'm far more comfortable thinking about my friends' issues than my own. Open my eyes and my child's to where we fall short. Prompt us to acknowledge where we're struggling, even where sin is gaining the upper hand—and call out to you for help. Remind us that you are always ready to answer our call, and wash us in your redeeming love. Amen.

MAKING IT PERSONAL

What sin do you struggle with that you've never told anyone else about? How does it keep you coming back to the Savior?

_____

_____

_____

_____

_____

_____

_____

_____

MAKING IT RELEVANT

For younger children: Jesus loves you, no matter how you act. But how do you think he wants you to act?

For older children: What happens to a person who is struggling with a sin but not confronting it, in their own heart or with friends? Do you have any sins that you worry will rule your life more than God does?

Day 26

I pray that when you are
broken—you'll discover that,
in healing, you grow stronger.

For this is what the high and lofty One says—
     he who lives forever, whose name is
     holy:
"I live in a high and holy place,
     but also with him who is contrite and
     lowly in spirit,
to revive the spirit of the lowly
     and to revive the heart of the contrite."

—Isaiah 57:15

Perhaps nothing breaks a mama's or papa's heart like hearing a child weep. Not from being upset or angry, but from being legitimately hurt. We feel our children's pain, their anxiety, their "lost-ness," and we long to fix whatever is breaking them. But sometimes we know they simply have to endure. Get through it. And trust that in time, they will find healing.

No one wishes for brokenness, and frankly, I'm not eager to experience it again—in my life or my child's. But looking back, the broken times in my life mark the seasons when the soil of my heart was tilled, most fertile for growth. There's something about feeling lost and unsure that sends us running to God for direction and reassurance. And when there's nothing else of substance to cling to and nothing else makes sense, we hear the echo of a call that has sounded in our hearts from birth: We belong to him. *You are mine. I am yours.*

In those intense times of brokenness—when we are desperate, pleading, spinning—we connect with our Lord *as* Lord of our lives. And the same is true for our children when we point them to the Comforter and Healer rather than trying to make it all better ourselves. When we allow them to go through the pain rather than trying to find a way around it.

My eldest experienced a measure of brokenness when she lost her sweet cousin Mady. The only soothing balm I could apply was the constant refrain, "We'll see her again. She's safe in heaven and happier than ever, waiting for us there. We're sad here, without her, and we're always going to miss her. But in time, life will feel okay again." Olivia was only seven when that happened, and could only process so much at that tender age, but her grief was real. She dreamed about her cousin. Cried over her. For years.

A decade later, I think Liv has a more solid understanding than most teens about the precious gift of life and the promises awaiting us in heaven. I think she has a wisdom borne from experiencing pain and recognizing that, in time, the pain recedes and joy returns. In other words, she is stronger than she would have been without the brokenness.

Would I trade that growth and maturity to get Mady back? Absolutely. A thousand times over. But we live in a world of brokenness. Sin. Death. Separation. Disease. And we trust in a God who brings joy and healing, even in the midst of horrific pain. We believe in a God who wants the best for us and can use all things—even brokenness—to bring us closer to him. When dark times come, we can trust his strong arms to hold us as we weep and to set us on our feet again, giving us his strength to move forward in faith.

Healer, life sometimes hurts. I spin and wonder how you could have let it happen, why you would. But I know you can use all things for your good, and I submit my heart to you. To mend the fractures and tend to my wounds. You know what it is to be broken. To feel abandoned and endure pain beyond measure. Give me strength when I have to

> *support my child as he suffers through his own*
> *time of brokenness. Give me the words that*
> *will point him to you. Help each of us to*
> *draw nearer to you in our shared pain, so*
> *that we might emerge from the valley stronger*
> *in our faith and ready to share in your joy.*
> *Amen.*

MAKING IT PERSONAL

Describe the last time you felt broken. What did healing look like in that situation?

_____

_____

_____

_____

_____

_____

_____

MAKING IT RELEVANT

For younger children: When we're sad, how does God heal us?

For older children: How can we draw closer to Jesus when we suffer? How does suffering help us better understand him?

Day 27

I pray you'll press through heartbreak—and be better able to identify true love.

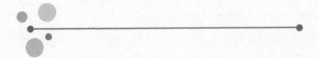

> The righteous cry out, and the LORD hears them;
> he delivers them from all their troubles.
> The LORD is close to the brokenhearted
> and saves those who are crushed in spirit.

—Psalm 34:17–18

My teen is in love. Last summer she was like a cartoon character, bouncing from one cloud to another on tiptoe, face alight, constantly smiling. This summer, she's more settled in her love for The Boy, and he in his for her. It seems steady and strong and solid. Maybe resilient enough to go the distance, even with him leaving for college this fall.

But I find myself guarding my own heart. Encouraging them both, but not allowing myself to fully believe this is the start of happily ever after. I, too, was once seventeen and deeply in love. Convinced I should get married as fast as possible. Hardly wanting to bother with college because all that mattered was Being Together.

Granted, my own relationship sported far more red flags and warning signs than I see in Olivia's. But, long story short, my first love eventually broke my heart into smithereens. And that heartbreak is one of the top ten things I'm grateful for. Yeah. Read that again. I am *so* glad my own boyfriend broke my heart.

There are several reasons for that. One, it forced me to rely on God in a whole new way. I sought him out as my Sustainer and Restorer and Lover of my soul when I was in a dark and lonely and broken place. And he answered my call, again and again, soothing me, drying my tears, and in time, healing me. The second reason is that it spared me from entering a marriage that would undoubtedly have been difficult, a relationship that would have demanded constant work rather than yielding pleasure and partnership. And I'm grateful that it helped me better understand who might be the best fit for me as a husband. That identification process helped draw Tim and me together, and we were married within a year of meeting, having both become stronger through the demise of previous relationships. Because we knew who we sought... and who we didn't.

The problem is that if we've suffered heartbreak, a part of us fears seeing our children go through the same pain. Some of us prop up relationships that aren't the best, dismiss red flags and soothe fears, all as part of our strategy of avoidance. Others of us wave those red flags in our children's faces, fearing they're headed toward greater heartache—and often unintentionally sending them right into their loved one's arms.

None of us can fail by pointing our children toward the Lover of their souls and encouraging them to seek his guidance, his model of true love, and see if their own relationship is a suitable reflection of it.

My daughter may very well be a young bride in a few years, and the groom at the end of the aisle may very well be The Boy. Or she may head down a completely different path, perhaps even embracing joyful singleness. Whatever happens, I am confident that God uses all things for good. Even heartbreak. If we let him.

Lover of my soul, you know how I hunger for love in my own life. I thank you for showing me your love through the people around me—my spouse, children, and friends.

> *Sustain my marriage, heal our rifts, build*
> *upon brokenness. And give my child the*
> *fortitude to pay attention to any red flags*
> *in her own relationship and the strength to*
> *resolve them, trusting you will always lead*
> *her toward the truest of loves. Amen.*

MAKING IT PERSONAL

Did you ever suffer a broken heart, before or during marriage?
What did you *gain* from the experience?

_____

_____

_____

_____

_____

_____

MAKING IT RELEVANT

For younger children: Do you know that God already knows
whether you will get married and, if so, who it will be? If you
get married, what do you think he or she will be like?

For older children: How would you describe your ideal girl-
friend/boyfriend? Are those the same things you'd look for in
a spouse?

Day 28

I pray you'll confront evil—
and recognize that Good is
a stronger force.

For our struggle is not against flesh and
blood, but against the rulers, against the
authorities, against the powers of this dark
world and against the spiritual forces of
evil in the heavenly realms.

—Ephesians 6:12

I mentioned in a previous devotional that a robber once put a gun to my head.

I was thirteen. We'd just come home from dinner out, and my younger brother and I were getting ready for bed. The dog barked. There was a knock at the door. My dad answered it and found a young couple on our doorstep, asking for directions. He got a map and took it to the door to show them. They hit him over the head with a gun and entered our home.

Wondering who had arrived, I went to the top of the stairs. The man rushed up, gun drawn, eyes wild. He grabbed my left arm and put the gun to my right temple. "Get down on the floor, or I'll kill you," he said.

I lay down. My brother was brought to lie beside me. We were tied up. They ransacked the house, looking for guns, cash, silver to support what we later learned was a fierce drug habit. My dad pretended we had no silver. My mother was hiding. My little brother whispered that he should try to escape and go after the only weapon he had—his X-Acto knife. And each time they passed us, I waited for a bullet to enter my back. I wondered if it would hurt. What it would feel like to die. Our dog came and laid down at our heads, clearly knowing something was very, very wrong but as helpless as we were to stop it.

Lying there in that hallway, I knew evil. I felt its presence every time the man walked by, like a frigid wave of air, so penetrating it literally made me shiver. But I also felt God's presence, like a circle of protection around us, pushing back the cold with warmth. Encouraging us. Reminding us that he was present even in that moment. I think he used our dog to be with us so we'd know we weren't alone.

Eventually, the robbers took off with their loot, thankfully leaving us alive. But for many months afterward, every time I walked through the hallway where we were held, I felt a chill to my bones, a combination of frightening memories and, I believe, the echo of evil in our home. That year, I learned that the spiritual realm is tangible, real. That a battle is taking place beyond what we can see, a battle with eternal ramifications. And that awakening has shaped my adult spiritual life—making it far more vibrant and important and vital to me than if I'd never brushed up against evil.

I want to prepare my children for their first recognition of evil and let them know that the Spirit arms them with all they need to do battle against it. This goes against our parental grain, doesn't it? We like to shield our children from even recognizing there are bad people in the world—and people who will specifically come for them, taking aim at their faith. But sometimes in our shielding, we leave them more at risk, vulnerable in their belief that they can live solely by their own strength. And if they are not aware of evil, how can they fully recognize God's good and mighty power? Without tasting sour, you cannot fully define sweet. Without feeling cold, you cannot fully appreciate warmth. Without knowing dark, you cannot fully comprehend light.

No sane mama would pray for a life-threatening encounter for her kids in order for them to realize they play a crucial role in the Lord's army. But I *am* praying that my children are awakened, aware, awash in the knowledge that God is with them, always, no matter what evil comes their way.

> *Prince of Peace, I get so lost in the day-to-day routine of life that I forget the constant, epic, unseen battle going on all around me. I understand so little of that realm, but I know you want me to be a warrior in prayer, in faith. I know you want us to lean on the sword of truth and lead others to understand that it does not all end here, on earth. Teach me and my children how to be aware of evil, to call it out and to rely on you to eradicate it. You are mighty, good, and true, Lord. Greater than any who are against us. And we draw strength from the fact that we are yours. Amen.*

MAKING IT PERSONAL

Where and when have you brushed up against evil?

_____

_____

_____

_____

_____

Making It Relevant

For younger children: What do you think God wants us to do about evil people?

For older children: Do you see people at school who you think are captured by the evil one? How might you reach out to them as a person of peace and grace and love and hope?

Day **29**

I pray you'll have to let go of a dream—and live to discover new ones.

Trust in the LORD with all your heart
and lean not on your own
understanding;
in all your ways acknowledge him,
and he will make your paths straight.

—Proverbs 3:5–6

I'm a dreamer and an entrepreneur and a novelist, so I spend a good portion of every day in my own little visionary world. I like to think about the "what if…" and build from there, from the foundation to the fruition. I've dreamed of companies and ministries and books—from little children's books to full-blown fictional series with a huge cast of characters and epic storylines. I've also dreamed of more personal things. Finding the right man to marry. Having children. Owning a house. Getting a dog. Discovering heart-friends.

My children are constantly dreaming of the future too, be it a change to their room décor, going on a youth trip, finding a job, dating someone, going to college, becoming a wedding planner, a chef, a pilot… On and on it goes. And the beauty of being a kid is that everything seems possible, right? We raise our children to believe they can accomplish anything they set their mind to. If they just work hard enough, have enough faith in themselves, it will happen. And we've witnessed enough success stories to make us all believers.

But sometimes the dream doesn't work out. You get fired or laid off. The restaurant closes. You can't get enough funding to launch the project. The college sends a rejection letter. You never meet the right guy. You struggle with infertility. There aren't enough people coming to keep your church doors open.

Some unrealized dreams we can shrug off. Others rake us over the coals in agony. We end up on our knees asking God,

Why, Lord, why? Why don't you bless me with this? Why don't you give me what I most crave? What I need? We think our lives incomplete without the fairy-tale ending. The "perfect" answer we expected.

I read once that God answers in three ways: *Yes, no,* or *not now.* We dreamers—even if we're subtle, closet-dreamers—expect the yes from God, don't we? We hope for it, against hope. Squinching up our eyes, crossing our fingers, and wishing for the best. But in that, are we hoping for luck rather than trusting that our God is holding us in his hands? And when God gives us the firm no—or the less obvious "not now"—we're taken aback. We struggle against it. My own inclination is to wrestle back control of the dream and *make it happen,* regardless of what God wants.

But I'm trying to develop the capacity to take the nos and the not-nows in stride—confident that God has something greater for me around the bend, either in a new dream or in seeing the dream flourish in a different time or different place. Or the "something greater" may simply be (and this is the hardest thing for me to swallow) in the waiting and trusting. That's the key, I find: the trust. The utter, overriding, complete confidence that God has my best interests in mind, and he's out to bring me closer to him, above any other goal. If I'm out to get closer to him, above any other goal or dream, then I'll set aside my own desires and pursue his.

As parents, we may try to keep our child from dreaming, discouraging them with practicalities in an effort to shield them from potential disappointment or failure. Or conversely, we might try to nurture a dream that ought to be allowed to die, fearing that its loss may devastate a child. If, instead, we can encourage our children to embrace the nos and not-nows, knowing the right yes is ahead, we will prepare them to live hopeful, optimistic, trusting, inspired lives.

> *Creator, you created each of us with a measure of vision. I know that sometimes I take visionary impulses and run with them to my own conclusion rather than yours. Then when your answer doesn't mesh with mine, I get upset. Forgive me, Lord, for trying to control and manage my own life rather than wholly trusting you to lead me where I am to go, when I am to go, how I am to go. Allow me to accept it when my children's dreams aren't realized and help them accept it too. Teach us how to be optimistic, and yet hold everything in our lives with open hands. Amen.*

MAKING IT PERSONAL

Has God ever disappointed you with an unrealized dream?
What good things occurred that might not have taken place
if your original dream had been realized?

_____

_____

_____

_____

_____

_____

_____

_____

MAKING IT RELEVANT

For younger children: What do you want to be when you grow
up? Do you think that's what God wants you to do?

For older children: Why do you think that God sometimes
says no, or not now, rather than yes, to our dreams or deep
desires?

Day **30**

I pray you'll watch a friendship fade—and discover the value of heart-friends who go the distance.

Therefore, as God's chosen people, holy and dearly loved, clothe yourselves with compassion, kindness, humility, gentleness and patience. Bear with each other and forgive whatever grievances you may have against one another. Forgive as the Lord forgave you.

—Colossians 3:12–13

I well remember the agony of losing my best friend in middle school. The cold reality of a girl—someone I thought would be a longtime friend—turning her back on me in favor of others. The heartsick wish that she'd taken me with her as she got swept up into the cool crowd. The discovery of a hateful note, making fun of me, and how that made me weep in private. The physical pain I got in my gut every time I saw her in the hallways, ignoring me as if I'd never been anything at all to her.

My girls have gone through it too—from sleepovers filled with laughter and shared secrets to the long, cold silence and colder shoulder. It brings the hurt back around again, but over and over I pray the same thing for them. *Bring them heartfriends, Lord. Friends who believe in you. Friends whom they can encourage, and in turn, friends who will encourage them to be more like you created them to be.* Although part of me longs to see all friendships restored, I know that losing unworthy friends makes space for deeper relationships. And living through the death of a friendship teaches us what true friendship and faithfulness are all about.

I wonder if you, like me, have been blessed with just a few rare friendships that go the distance? It takes work, but we are able to cultivate and maintain the friendships that matter, even as years and physical distance and busy lives pull us apart. The friends who are loyal, who understand and support us as much as we do them, who are intent on pursuing a deeper relationship with Christ as well as with us—those are the friendships we ought to fight hard to keep. But too often we settle for the obvious and the comfortable in friendships, as we do in so many areas of our lives. We ease into the casual relationship that keeps us entertained and busy but doesn't push or challenge or make us think. God calls us to be "as iron sharpens iron" (Proverbs 27:17), and that rarely happens in the casual relationship.

So sometimes the loss of a friendship can be a blessing in disguise. It makes us more cautious and choosy in reaching out to others, and prompts us to think about the kind of friends God might call us toward. People of integrity as well as fun. People who are living out their faith, inspiring us to do the same. People in whom we can invest, as they invest in us, truly embodying the word *sister* or *brother*.

And if we can teach our children how to seek out those kinds of friends too, they'll be able to build Christ-centered friendships and know the blessing of a spiritual family, something that can be stronger than even blood kin.

> *Lover of all, I want to make room for the people who will make my life richer and more meaningful. You designed us for deep connection. Help me to get past old hurts and venture into trusting the new, godly people you bring into my life. Give me the energy to make the time to get to know them. Bring us together in ways that solidify our relationship. And while I want my children to shine your*

> *love to everyone, help them differentiate be-*
> *tween friends and heart-friends. Help them to*
> *let the unhealthy relationships go and invest*
> *in those that would delight you, Lord. Amen.*

MAKING IT PERSONAL

Have you ever lost a friend? What insights did you gain from that experience? What do you think God is telling you about your need for friends?

_____

_____

_____

_____

_____

_____

_____

_____

MAKING IT RELEVANT

For younger children: What makes a good friend?

For older children: How do you think God defines friendship? What kind of person do you think he wants you to have as a best friend?

Day 31

I pray you'll one day pray over a child of your own—and know more about why you're a beloved, treasured child yourself.

For you did not receive a spirit that makes you a slave again to fear, but you received the Spirit of sonship. And by him we cry, "*Abba*, Father." The Spirit himself testifies with our spirit that we are God's children.

—Romans 8:15–16

This last upside-down devotional isn't about what we can teach our children as much as it is about what our children can teach us and, in turn, what their children will teach them. As my kids grow up and I see glimpses of the future women and future man they are becoming, I have occasional thoughts about grandchildren. I have some years left before that will happen (I hope!), but the tender thoughts make me smile. A baby in the house is always fun. But it's even more enjoyable to look ahead to what my children will learn through their own parenting experiences. Because when we become parents, we conversely learn new things about what it is to be a child...a child of God.

Becoming a parent changed so many things for me at a fundamental level. Getting pregnant and experiencing the growth of my child in the womb brought me face to face with the miracle of how life begins and our Creator's hand in it. (Something my friends who've struggled with infertility came to understand in even greater depth.) The fact that the hospital let us—inexperienced us!—walk out with this fragile being in our arms brought home responsibility in a whole new way. Spending weeks sleep-deprived and bleary-eyed taught us selflessness. Enduring tantrums taught us true patience. Enforcing discipline encouraged us to focus on our children's greater good and our long-term goals for them, even in the midst of temporary discomfort and pain.

I've watched friends nurse chronically ill children for weeks, months, years, body-weary but tireless in their tenacity and tenderness. I've watched others fight for their children—

for justice, for opportunity, for grace, for another chance—
and when they were older, encourage their children to rise
and fight on their own. I've watched moms and dads pray on
their knees, brokenhearted over the prodigal and beaming
with joy over kids walking the walk.

All of those lessons have taught me more about how my
God sees and cares for *me.* Just as I love and treasure my children, so does he treasure and love me. Just as I sacrifice to give
them what they need and find pleasure in giving them the
"little bit extra," so does he, with me. I delight in them, just as
he delights in me (Psalm 18:19; 147:11). Zephaniah 3:17 tells
us that "The LORD your God is with you.... He will take
great delight in you, he will quiet you with his love, he will
rejoice over you with singing."

How often does my love for my kids feel like singing in
my heart? Okay, truth be told, there are many days when
their actions don't really make me feel like singing. But there
have been many precious, tender moments when my love for
them feels like a piercing of my heart. It is so intense, so true,
so all-encompassing that I know that nothing—nothing—
could ever make me *not* love them. They are forever my own.
Just as I, in turn, am claimed and loved forever by my heavenly Father.

It is my hope that my kids will someday pray upside-
down prayers for their own children, teaching them to be
confident, courageous disciples who wholly trust the God
they serve. The God who loves them. The God who calls
them his precious children. And I pray my grandchildren will

raise their children to do the same. In this way each of us will leave the finest legacy possible on this earth: children who know they belong to their Creator, first, and their family, second. In such a family, God can do mighty things, indeed.

> *Father God, thank you for loving me as your child. Thank you for loving my children even more than I do, impossible as that is to imagine. I pray that you will bless them with their own children someday, so that they might see these lessons of love and discover greater depth in their faith, through the lessons you teach us in that special parent-child relationship. Amen.*

MAKING IT PERSONAL

What's the biggest lesson being a parent has taught you about God?

_____

_____

_____

_____

_____

_____

MAKING IT RELEVANT

For younger children: How is God like a mommy or a daddy?

For older children: What do you think is a parent's most important task? How is that similar to the way God parents each of us?

ACKNOWLEDGMENTS

My sincere thanks go out to...

Scharlotte Rich, who taught me my very first upside-down prayer as a parent. Thanks for prompting me to think outside the box and learn to pray that it's best for my kids to get caught doing something wrong *early,* rather than later.

Alice Crider, for sharing the vision that a blog post could actually become a book.

Laura Barker, for adopting the vision and pushing to make it much more than it was at delivery. Much, *much* more.

And the entire WaterBrook team, for designing a gorgeous cover and getting it out into the world, on bookstore shelves and into readers' hands.

I appreciate you all.